Contents

Why "The Ardor of Hope"?

How to capture a complete book in fourteen letters and four words? By distilling the message down to its essence.

Hope happens when we know there is more, are confident we could make it happen, recognize the steps to achieve it, and feel its results within our grasp.

Ardor is the passion that fires the hope to create; the electricity that causes the affect; the voltage that charges the change.

The Ardor of Hope is a dream energized efficiently, an idea plugged into a power source, a belief in your self, supported by a plan to get there.

Why Write a Book?

We wrote this book for ourselves—with the hope that the world may eavesdrop.

We wrote this book not to seek all of the answers, rather, some of the questions. We constructed these pages spending little time worrying about destinations and much time enjoying the journey.

This book started as an exploration—and ended as one as well.

We aspired more than we conspired. We aspired to understand the oneness in the multitude; we did not conspire to define it.

There are trillions of cells in the human body. There are billions of human bodies on planet earth. There are countless planets in existence. What is its spark? Is there something that ties it all together? How is there hope in the seemingly hopeless vastness?

With so much going on, where is the vision and unison—the hope and the ardor—to make it all happen? Is it here, there, or everywhere?

We wrote *The Ardor of Hope* to look for it more than find it; to provide tools and materials more than ready-made appointments; to tease possibilities more than calculate probabilities. In writing *The Ardor of Hope* we simply wanted to leave no stone unlearned.

It is our ardor and our hope that you enjoy reading this book as much as we enjoyed writing it.

Our greatest gift would be that you read *The Ardor of Hope* with open eyes. And, as you come upon its final drops of ink, you find that your eyes are more open yet.

Thank you for reading.

~~

Every new beginning is challenging.
Every challenge brings a new beginning.

CHAPTER ONE

Fire

Truth is a bonfire:
It moves continuously;
It burns upwardly;
It sparks outwardly.

~~

Fire Engine

It is a beautiful thing, to watch it dance and flicker. It burns hot and true, always leaping upward, never standing still. Its power is humbling: It can forge opposites, just as easily as it can divide mountains. It can turn darkness to light, but it can also turn lightness into dark ash.

It is called Fire and it is all-consuming. It is called Fire and it is the engine of the world.

The Fire is contagious. Anything that comes close catches fire too. The Fire breathes deeply, feeding off the oxygen of the world. It inhales raw material, and exhales pure energy.

What would you give to know such a fire? What would you sacrifice to tap into such an awesome power? How far would you travel to feel such heat? How much would you pay to possess such light?

No matter how far you travel, how much you give, how much you sacrifice, or how much you pay, you will never find this fire. Indeed, the farther away you look, the farther away the fire will be.

You see, dear friend, this fire lives within you. The only way to find this fire is to find your true self. This fire is who you are.

Together, let us ignite its spark and spark its curiosity.

Fire Pump

Being born is being kindled. The mere fact that you exist means that the universe is a warmer and more illuminated place for it. It is as simple and profound as that.

Your fire is a gift from a power greater than yourself. You did not ask for this fire, but you have the power to answer its calling. As with all gifts, the important question is not, *Why was it given to me?* But rather, *What am I going to do with it?* The answer to this question, what you are going to do with the fire, is the reason the fire was given to you.

The fire's calling is to burn—and burn is what you will do.

Every man, woman, and child is a fire. But no two fires are the same. Each and every fire burns with its exacting heat, its unique light, its special dance, its distinctive harmony of colors and textures.

Of all the fires that have ever burned in the past, of all the fires that burn in the present, and of all the fires that will burn in the future, no fire can burn the way your fire can burn. Your fire is exclusive to you, and it is irreplaceable.

No person can take this fire away from you because no person gave it to you. The people in your life can help you fan the flames, or they can move out of the way before they get burned. Trying to put out someone's fire is like trying to turn a diamond into a clump of dirt. It is not going to happen.

No matter how much someone tries to douse your flame—and unfortunately this world is often a cold and dark place—your flame will always flicker on and upward. No thing or person can extinguish your fire, because no thing or person sparked your fire.

Though the fire is always there, oftentimes it can be concealed. Sometimes we are hurt so deeply, life feeling like an endless frozen winter, that it seems as if it the fire has gone out completely.

But always know this: Just as the flame is at times concealed within the black coal, so is your fire at times concealed within the black coal of life. All that is required, though, is to fan the coal; then the fire within it will leap up, burning bright and true in a revealed way for all to see and feel.

The purpose of these words is to act as a bellows. Direct it at the coals, press down, and blow until the embers reappear, then flicker, then flame.

The spark of fire is always there. Sometimes we just need the match of memory to help us ignite it.

Firepower

This fire is your single greatest gift, and your single greatest power. Indeed, this fire is the source of all your power, allowing you to accomplish anything you like. For your fire, no dream is too improbable and no goal is deemed unreachable. Your fire can help you trail-blaze any path you truly believe in.

Your incredible successes are contingent on this fire, as are your incredible failures. The difference between success and failure is how much you allow your fire to burn. Success happens when you set yourself on fire, tapping into the fire's awesome power; failure happens when you either do not realize that you have this firepower, or are too afraid to let it burn. Perhaps you are even afraid that your fire might burn you.

But you yourself are fire. Can fire itself get burned?

Fire is energy. Energy is the number-one ingredient for any success. A fire is single-minded; it needs to burn and uses anything in its path as fuel. A fire is contagious; whatever it touches becomes fire too. And a fire is alive, feeding off the oxygen to grow and accomplish its mission.

The same holds true with your fiery energy, your energetic fire: It is single-minded in its goal to move forward and upward, transforming everything in its path to fuel for its purpose. The energy of your fire is contagious; whatever it touches becomes energized too. And your fire is alive, breathing in the oxygen of the world to grow and accomplish your purpose.

Imagine that a burning fire suddenly stops and loses focus—it is impossible, it just does not happen. Fires never get distracted. Fires turn distraction into attraction, gaining traction, setting distractions ablaze. Losing focus is a major factor in never reaching your goal. Your fire never allows you to lose your focus. Your fire turns distraction into fuel to burn brighter and hotter, to reach your goal even faster.

Fires do not analyze. Fires burn. Sure, we need our minds and intellects to analyze the paths we wish to journey upon. But it is the fire that gets us to the destination. An automobile has a Global Positioning System to map its direction, but the engine alone makes the car drive. Your fire is your engine, empowering your journey through life.

The map that is your mind is there for you to use; it is not there for it to use you. If all you do is analysis, that is rather similar to paralysis. This would be akin to a car with a state-of-the-art GPS but no engine. The journey will constantly be recalculating.

The breakthrough occurs when the GPS of your mind is conflagrated by the inferno of your fiery soul. This is called combustion, and it can drive you to places beyond your wildest dreams.

Fire Tempered

But wild dreams are not enough. There are fires that burn things down, down to the ground, and there are fires that burn things up, up to the heavens. What will ensure that your fire illuminates and warms without obliterating and destroying?

A fire has the ability to forge bonds between two opposites, welding the links in a chain; but a fire also has the ability to shatter things that are whole. A fire can solder cracks, or create them.

The difference between a constructive fire and a destructive one is control. By tempering, conducting, and harnessing the fire, you optimize its power in the most productive and efficient manner.

Fire's nature is to rage relentlessly. Because of its infinite potential, fire requires subtlety and respect, more than any other factor in your life. Fires are never neutral. Either they are lighting things up or they are burning things down.

Channeling the flames is the difference between a tender hug and a scolding slap. It is the difference between getting warm and getting burned. It is the difference between being illuminated and being blinded.

Imagine trying to boil water for tea with a raging forest fire. Sure, the water will boil—but so will the kettle and everything else. It will boil and burn until nothing is left.

But cultivating that same fire upon a stovetop allows you to boil a kettle of water until it whistles in delight. Both the forest fire and the stove fire are hot; only the former is out of your control while the latter is in your control. The latter allows you to brew a glass of tea, but the former does not allow you to brew anything.

You can temper your fire in so many different ways and in so many different directions. Control allows you to hone your fire to be the most productive energy possible.

Fire or Smoke?

If you have ever built a fire, you know that some fires burn cleanly and effortlessly, while others burn in jagged disarray and give off acrid smoke. The difference between these two fires is that one is built upon clean and

appropriate fuel, while the other is founded upon materials that are not conducive—even harmful—for burning.

Have you ever gone camping? You build a beautiful and warm bonfire and it flickers in peaceful serenity. Then, for no apparent reason, some genius decides to roll a rubber tire into the bonfire. What was once a haven of light and warmth has now become a prison of poisonous fumes and asphyxiating smoke.

It is often the case that we use life's past experiences to fuel our future successes. We may use pain as an example. Pain is a very acute and personal feeling. Many people use pain as a catalyst for growth and prosperity. Pain can be a great lever for any passion. One might say that the greater the pain, the greater the gain and the greater the fire it fuels.

But if all you have is pain, and your fire for life is only built upon pain, then sooner or later that fire will begin to smoke. Pain is a great catalyst for discovering your true intrinsic fire, but pain is not meant to be your intrinsic fire.

Your intrinsic fire, the natural state of your pure being, is devoid of any artificial substance. There are no rubber tires, no plastic bottles, and no harmful pollutants floating around in your essential bonfire. It burns true and forever without any superficial starter or chemical accelerator.

A fire that is completely contingent upon an external force, like pain, will sooner or later fill its rooms with smoke, it will permeate every experience with a tar-like toxicity, and the pollutants from the jagged emotion of brokenness will snuff out the organic growth that sustains our lives. We must never allow our pain to create our purpose. We may only allow our pain to fuel and awaken it. Pain can motivate, but pain will never sustain.

It is the all-consuming essential fire alone that has the power to burn brightest without ever polluting the air we breathe.

To take it one step further: At a certain point in life our bodies begin to wither and fade. Everything physical must die, and the body is very physical. Yet we ignore this atrophy, choosing to live as if we will live forever, believing, hoping, that there is something more.

Which one is it? Does everything die or is there eternality?

These two paradoxical feelings stem from the two paradoxical ingredients of our being, our fire and our smoke. Our bodies are like smoke, and our souls are like fire. When your body is one with your soul, your body gives off very little smoke and burns clean and pure. But when the body tries to burn on its own, forgetting the fire of its soul, then the body begins to smoke like a smoldering tire. It suffocates, it is toxic, and it is unbearable.

Smoke, at a certain point, fades away, leaving less than a cloud of memory. So too do bodies. After a certain amount of time, they fade away into the mists of time.

True fires, however, burn forever. Sure, at a certain point when the body fades and there no longer is a vehicle upon which to burn, the fire seems to have gone out. But, in truth, the fire burns perpetually and eternally. At a certain point one may be unable to touch the fire's wick, but one can always feel the fire's warmth.

You must differentiate between the things in life that are genuine fire and the things that are but fleeting smoke. The fire is everlasting; the smoke fades away. Not always is there fire where there is smoke and, if we achieve what our potential allows us to achieve, there won't be smoke where there is fire.

Firemen and Women

The difference between a leader and a follower is the ability to differentiate between fire and smoke, and the ability to harness the fire in the most maximizing way.

This transforms an ordinary person into an extraordinary person. There are great people, for whom the fire burns openly and fiercely. You look at them and you see their light and feel their warmth. We call these people leaders, visionaries, and inspirations.

We too, you and I, can each be one of these people. All we have to do is access our fire, harness it, and supply it with pure, clean fuel.

There is but one difference between a leader and follower. It is called Fire! Have you ever seen a fire follow? No. Fires do not follow; fires lead.

You are a fire. All you have to do is burn. You are a leader. All you have to do is lead.

Fireplace

Fires work best in environments that are conducive for their natural growth. Fires need air, fires need fuel, fires need care, fires need love, fires need structure, fires need respect, and fires need space.

A hearth—a fireplace—is the perfect home for a fire because it has airflow, it has containment, it is centralized, it is dry and, very importantly, a fireplace allows for its fire to be enjoyed and appreciated. Come now, there is nothing quite like sitting around a fireplace, basking in the collective warmth with the people you love.

You can know whether your fire is in the right place by watching the way it burns. If your fire is struggling to flourish, perhaps it is time to change your environment, or influences, or materials. Sometimes you have to pick yourself up and move to a different place, be it a literal material move or a figurative spiritual move.

The airflow, vented by your will and desire, directs your consuming flame. The more air, the hotter the fire; the stronger the wind, the further the fire reaches. The airflow is contingent on the fire's place and position. If you bury your fire beneath mountains of dirt, every flicker of your fire will be a painful struggle. But if your fire's place is within a nurturing hearth, then oh, how beautiful and warm it will burn.

When your fire is in a healthy environment, that environment, too, becomes fiery and bright, healthy and holistic.

At a certain seminal point, it becomes difficult to differentiate between your inner fire and the outer fire it inspires.

At this flashpoint, you know that you have come to the right fireplace.

Firelight

Fire is the ability to light up the world, to illuminate everyone you meet and everything you touch. This light is a gift that has been given to you by something greater than yourself—it has been gifted to you by Light itself.

Light, like fire, is a transformative experience. A goldsmith uses fire to turn gold into liquid, and liquid gold into shapes. A glassblower uses the furnace to melt the glass, until it is pliable enough to form. A blacksmith uses the fire to link the iron chains and mend the seemingly indelible cracks.

And so do you and I. The human being uses his or her fire to melt the iron cynicism of the world, making it pliable so that he or she may shape this earth into a beautiful garden. Fire allows us to take anything, no matter how big or how small, no matter how precious or how cheap, no matter how strong or how weak, and turn it into something better than itself.

We use fire to turn darkness to light. And we use fire to mend hearts, weld rifts, and create fusion where before there was only fission.

Fire and light are miraculous. The reward is so much greater than the investment. One tiny candle can illuminate an entire cellar of darkness. And a single candle provides light for one person as it does for one hundred people.

This is the beauty of fire, and light: Sharing it increases, never diminishes, its power. When two fires meet they do not fight with one another, by-and-by becoming weaker, but they unite together and become stronger. Put two good fires together and it becomes one great fire. Put two great fires together and it becomes one greater fire.

Your fire—and the firelight it exudes—is more powerful than any atom. Your fire has the ability to transform any atom, providing it with a whole new light. Human beings have the ability to rearrange the furniture of this planet. We can take two molecules and build with them an empire; we can take an empire and build with it a universe. We do this through tapping into the fire that burns within our souls.

Our fires drive every cell, nuance, limb, and system of our bodies to nurture (or uproot) the garden here on this planet.

You do not choose the fire within you. You only choose whether it will be a fire that illuminates the cosmic garden or a fire that eliminates all possibility for growth.

Choose wisely.

Misfires and Backfires

Every passion known to humankind is an interpretation of the fire that lives within us. A passion for someone you love is your fire interpreted in the language of love; a passion for professional achievement is your fire interpreted in the language of work.

As such, we must take urgent care not to allow our fire to misfire or backfire, lest it translate into a passion for destructive things. Just as an individual's energy and passion may be directed into positive and healthy things, this same fiery passion could also be misdirected toward things that are unhealthy and detrimental.

The forms of misfired misdirection are many: abuse, addiction, anger, rage, unfaithfulness, hate, selfishness, and all of their synonyms. These are all misdirected currents that may carry one over the cliff of demise.

Directing your fiery passion for love in a healthy manner, with the sanctity, commitment, respect, and honor another human being deserves, is called intimacy. But misdirecting your fiery passion for love in an unhealthy, impure, or abusive manner is called pornography.

The former is a fire; the latter is a misfire.

Addiction is a fire controlling you, you not controlling it. Addiction begins with one small misfire, just as a forest fire begins with a single forgotten ember at an innocent campsite. But once the addiction or forest fire begins to take hold, it can take many weeks and untold damage before it burns out.

It is much easier to prevent a forest fire from starting in the first place than it is to extinguish it after it has already begun. So too with misfires: prevent them from sparking in the first place, as they are much harder to extinguish once they begin building momentum.

The greatest preemptive measure you can take is to focus your fire upon positive things. Then, every fire will be a good fire, never a misfire.

Fireworks

Today is a new day. Every morning the sun rises with new possibilities. And every morning your inner sun, your inner fire rises within you with new possibilities, saturating every fiber of your being in passion and energy for another bright and productive day.

Fire is never at a standstill. And neither is life. The mission of your soul is to constantly choose your life's course by igniting, every single day, the all-consuming fire within you. Even if yesterday wasn't such a fiery day, today will be. You have been mired in the mud for long enough. Stop fearing the worst and begin expecting the best. It is time to unleash your heat upon the world.

When you arise in the morning with this knowledge burning within you, it influences the far-reaches of your day and changes everything. Now, with the fire lit, you can begin to explore your professional dreams and financial freedoms. Today is the day you will use your fire to forge beautiful relationships. At this very moment, you will apply your fire to mending any hurts and welding together all of life's schisms.

There are two options in life: You can live feeling trapped and abused, or you can put match to wick and let the fireworks begin. Watch as your soul catches fire and burns through the chains of despair; feel the explosion of heat consuming every hindrance in your way, turning the obstacles into opportunities, turning the earth into a heaven, turning the fuel into energy, turning problems into solutions.

You may be thinking: Maybe I don't really need the fire; maybe all I need is some money to make me happy, some dollars to deal with my sense. Well, one thing is for certain: Money without purpose is worthless; money without fire is completely cold. You see, money cannot create your fire, but your fire can create money.

This is the biggest difference between your fire and everything else you possess. Your fire is internal and essential; everything else is external and optional. Your fire can always create everything else; everything else combined can never create your fire.

Fire works. All you have to do is light the fuse and enjoy the experience as it explodes in a dance of warmth and light.

~~

Like a soft smile or one kind word,
a fragile twig can kindle the mightiest of branches.

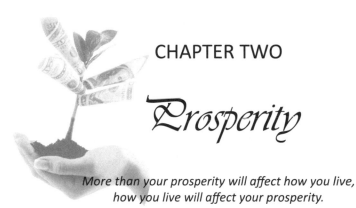

CHAPTER TWO

Prosperity

*More than your prosperity will affect how you live,
how you live will affect your prosperity.*

~~

Nature Calls

In its natural state, it never stops growing. If left to its own devices, it perpetually increases. If allowed to be, it prospers eternally. This is what a fire knows and this is how a fire burns. Pure energy is dynamic and constantly energetic. Pure fire prospers and never stops prospering.

Something must go terribly wrong for a fire to slow down, to struggle, or to diminish. Only if some foreign force, antithetical to energy and growth, is allowed into the fire's sphere—say the environment becomes harsh and stormy, or the fuel begins to run low—only then could the pure light be shuttered; only then could the warmth of its flame shudder.

At our nucleus, we are all fires. At our seminal selves, we are pure energy. At this essential level, we are in constant, perpetual, eternal pulsating prosperity. We can darken our burning light and restrict our natural warmth only if we introduce an external detrimental force into our fire's sphere.

The choice we face every moment of every day is to either allow our personal fires to prosper naturally, or to stifle their growth with unnatural restrictions. Only we and we alone can get in the way of our own fires and our own potential. And only we and we alone can ensure that we do not.

When the fire burns proud, we call it prospering. When the fire whimpers softly, we call it struggling.

The onus is upon us to rise to this challenge. And the challenge is twofold: First, we must learn to ensure that nothing harmful gets in the way of our natural fires, allowing them to prosper organically. Second, we must familiarize every element of our living with our essential fire by applying the innate fire to every aspect of our lives.

This, fires of the world, is the secret to prosperity. Connect to your fire, to your engine, to your natural state of flourishing and progression. And disconnect from all things that may decrease your passion and weaken your burn.

Self Help

Libraries of books have been published, universes of words have been written, and copious amounts of ink have been spilled in the name of prosperity. There are countless self-help gurus, infinite multitudes of life coaches, and numerous motivational speakers that will help you find prosperity for a few easy one-time cash payments—plus, of course, shipping and handling.

However, if achieving prosperity is as easy as joining a seminar or signing up for a life-changing retreat, why then do most of us struggle? Why then is most of the world not prospering?

There are a-million-and-one get-rich-quick schemes. But, for some reason, the only ones who seem to get rich quick from these schemes are those who

are selling them. If it is so quick and easy to prosper, why don't the gurus quit selling these schemes and go prosper?

Prospering is not easy. Prospering is living. And living never stops. Prospering is not something outside of your self. Prospering is something that lives inside your very core. Discovering the secret to your prosperity from someone else's ideas is not discovering your prosperity, but someone else's.

To find your unique prosperity, you must find your unique self. And to find your unique self, you must find your unique fire.

The first step in finding your unique fire is recognizing that you do not have to create your fire; you just have to remove the obstacles in its path. You do not have to create your prosperity; you have to merely remove the blockages that halt its progress.

Put a different way: the only form of self-help required in order to prosper is the kind that focuses more on the self and less on the help. As we come to discover, it is your very own self that is the greatest help you could ever need.

Aptitude for Attitude

A clichéd bumper sticker, clinging to the backside of the speeding automobile that is prosperity, exclaims in big, bold letters: POSITIVE ATTITUDE. This proverbial car graffiti purports that if you have a positive attitude you will prosper, and if you have a negative attitude you will struggle.

That is all very good and nice—in the realm of fantasy. But in this very real world in which we live, there are many successful multimillionaires who are just downright negative, just as there are many positive people that are treading the murky pools of poverty.

A cynic might even argue that the more positive your attitude the less prosperous you will be. Nice guys finish last, and only cold, hard sharks know how to navigate the stormy seas and negotiate a prosperous deal.

Positive attitude is indeed a positive thing to have; but positivity alone will

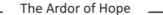
not discover prosperity—especially in a world bombarded with negativity and selfishness.

Short Cuts

Another big selling point for prosperity—and most things, for that matter—is the shortcut. If you buy this easy-to-read book, or watch this brief seminar, or study this quick curriculum, you will have the direct path to success. The problem with shortcuts is that by cutting through you miss everything else on the journey. The problem with shortcuts is that they are short and they cut.

Imagine the most beautiful orchard, interlaced with flawless streams clearer than a diamond, flowers in perfect bloom harmonizing with fruit bursting forth with the sweetest juices. Two paths lead through this beautiful orchard. The first path cuts right through and gets you to the other side without breaking your stride or attracting your eye. The second path passes through every single element existing in this orchard, zigzagging between the humbling flora, caressing the tranquil complexity, and capturing the pure innocence.

Which of these two paths would you choose to walk along? The first path will get you through the orchard in no time; while the second path will take you days, years, maybe even a lifetime to get to the other side. The second path will allow you to experience the beautiful orchard, while the first path will barely offer you a fleeting glance. The first path is about record time, while the second path is about recording time.

Life is a beautiful orchard, home to the most humbling symphonies known to humankind. Two paths run through life's living orchard. The first path looks for the easiest, shortest possible route through the beauty; the second path looks for the best possible route to capture and experience the beauty. Which path will you choose?

Prosperity is not getting to the other side as quickly as possible. Prosperity is walking through every detail of life and appreciating the greatest symmetries and the tiniest buds alike.

Shortcuts are short both in time and results. Prosperity is long both in work and outcomes. The two of them clash.

One question we would be wise to keep in mind when broached with a shortcut is: If I never experience the road itself how will I ever know the journey? Discovering prosperity is discovering prosperity, and no one ever discovered anything by taking a shortcut.

Life is a journey, and prosperity is recognizing, appreciating, and maximizing the many opportunities along the way. A fire does not prosper by seeking the shortest route to burn; a fire prospers by following the right path to burn.

Find the best possible path by knowing the roads, vehicles, ups, downs, U-turns, pit stops, gas stations, traffic patterns, on-ramps and exits of life.

If you do not know how to operate your vehicle, or if you do not recognize the road you are on, or if you are illiterate to the signposts along the way, or if you are blind to the beautiful landscapes flashing by how could the journey be anything but painful and miserable?

When, however, you recognize the road, are an expert driver, can read even the finest street sign print, and know to drink in every colorful detail of the landscape, the journey becomes exciting and beautiful.

To become an expert traveler, you have to learn how to travel. And to learn how to travel, you have to follow the directions.

Instructions to Follow

How often have we heard: *If only you would follow the rules, if only you would follow the directions, if only you would follow the instructions*? The moment we hear the word follow, our minds shut down and our hearts clamp up. We human beings do not like to follow anything. We like to lead.

This is why, when a man gets lost while driving in an unfamiliar neighborhood, he will never stop to ask for directions. This is also why a man will never follow the instructions when assembling an item he just bought. We do not like to follow; we do not like to be told what to do; we want to experiment and figure it out on our own.

But what happens if the instructions are not there to follow but to lead, to lead us to a greater appreciation and a greater understanding of the journey itself? Suddenly the instructions do not command us how to walk, but provide us with tools to fly.

Fires are not followers. Fires are leaders. Followers do not need instructions. Followers will simply follow. Leaders need instructions: instructions on how to lead; instructions on how to live, how to burn, how to blaze paths and ignite greatness.

Fires lead by adhering to certain principles. Fires need to prosper and they need fuel, oxygen, direction, care, and safety to do so. Your inner fire is no different. Certain principles and systems and instructions are necessary for you to prosper.

And the greater your fire—the greater your ambition and prosperity—the greater and more complex are the instructions required to achieve the perfect burn. Take any business as an example: the bigger and more sophisticated the business, the bigger and more sophisticated the guiding systems and directive structures streamlining the business.

Your prosperity is big business.

Buying into your fire's system and never wavering from its instructions is a big challenge. Often we will find ourselves trying to tell the fire how to burn instead of listening to the fire telling us how to burn. We want to preach to the fire's choir instead of listening to its chorus. However difficult it may be, and at times it will be very difficult, we must always be careful to lead by the instructions, and not try to lead the instructions.

Who ever said that experiencing the orchard of prosperity was easy?

For easy, you may have to go the shortcut route: for easy you may have to rush through to the other side of the orchard without reveling in the humbling beauty of the journey.

Instruction Site

Every single endeavor in the universe follows a certain set of instructions.

The laws of physics instruct matter; the rules of language instruct communication; the notes and scales of music direct the composition of song; the codes of computer programming instruct the innovative software.

The same is true for you and your life. There are specific instructions by which to prosper and succeed. Following these guidelines allows you to flourish in ways beautiful and artful. Obeying these rules is akin to a brilliant poet obeying the rules of language: the rules can set you free and allow you to become intimate with your fire.

Obedience has advantages over sacrifice. Sacrifice allows us to dedicate certain portions of ourselves to succeed and prosper; but obedience instructs us on which things to dedicate and which things to hold on to.

Instructions are very nuanced and exacting. You must follow them completely, coherently, and correctly. Otherwise, they don't work. This is not an easy task. Adhering to specific instructions is like building a multifarious space station—only more complex. But it also comes naturally to you, because it is part of your fire and your engine.

We all want to be clever. We all want to create new systems and new instructions, and new subjective navigational tools by which to compass our lives. But that would be like a writer creating a new alphabet, or a musician creating a new set of notes. That is not genius. Genius is taking the language, the structure, the instruction—and understanding it in such a deep way that you can utilize it to convey brilliance. That is true genius.

It is reminiscent of the great mystic who once saw a gentleman running down the street. The mystic stopped the gentleman and inquired as to where he was running. The gentleman responded that he is running to work, to make a living, to prosper. To which the mystic asked: How do you know you are running toward your prosperity and not away from your prosperity?

The instructions of life allow us to know and recognize when we are coming toward our fire and prosperity, and when we are moving away from it.

This means that prosperity is not the *result* of your work, but prosperity *is* your work. Your work is to study the instructions, apply them to your fire and goals, and implement them to the best of your abilities.

But where are these instructions? Where can they be found? Where are they hiding? Thankfully, they are right in front of you, pulsating within the manual of life.

Manual Labor

When you purchase a certain piece of merchandise, that item comes with a user guide or an instruction manual. The more complex the object, the more detailed the instructions are. A shirt merely has a few washing instructions: tumble dry low, or wash with like colors; a space shuttle takes years of intricate study to comprehend its nuanced manual.

If a shirt, or a space shuttle, requires an instruction manual to direct its prosperity, how much more so does a human life require a manual to teach us how to prosper? If your shirt requires a tag to instruct you how to best treat it, does your life need an instructive tag any less?

Assembling a piece of furniture can take you an hour; assembling your prosperous life takes all the days of your living.

Imagine purchasing a do-it-yourself bookshelf. It comes with all the required pieces but assembly is required. Included in the box is, naturally, an instruction manual. Because you are a pretty wise guy, you decide to forgo the manual and begin assembling this bookshelf by your own guidance. You lay out all the pieces and begin assembling.

Before long, your bookshelf starts to resemble a barstool. You put this screw where that peg was supposed to go and you put that board where this leg was supposed to go. Certainly, especially if you are handy, sooner or later you might figure it out. But in all likelihood, following the manual would be less time-consuming and less stressful.

Now imagine a team of NASA engineers trying to assemble a space shuttle. They have all the necessary pieces but decide to forgo the plans, blueprints, and instruction manual. The likelihood of that shuttle functioning is about zero, and no sane person would ever board that aircraft.

Certainly life, the most intricate of all intricacies, requires a manual to know how to assemble its many parts, appreciate its beauty, and allow it to flourish and prosper.

The manual of life is what we call: *The World's Book*.

The World's Book

The world is your manual, containing your instructions. Study the manual and prosper. Learn from all things and become informed. Be open to every creation's message, and welcome every pixel of existence, no matter how insignificant it may seem. Nothing—absolutely not one thing—is meaningless. The only meaningless thing is thinking that something may be meaningless.

Why does a fire simply burn to the best of its abilities and never asks: *What is the best way for me to burn?* Because fires are programmed this way and are not distracted by other things. So too the world is programmed this way, and it is not distracted by other things.

We humans, at times, may be so distracted by mundane superficialities that we may forget the fire that rages within, that prospers naturally; we may have been hurt so badly that we believe our fires have gone out. At times like these we must look to the world's book, the manual that instructs us on how to return to our natural light and inherent warmth.

When we look at the world, our manual, we must ask: *Do I want to be like this bird, soaring to the heavens; or do I want to be like that snake, slithering on its belly? Do I want to be like that sunshine, warming its constituents; or do I wish to be like that storm cloud, casting a shadow on the alleyway?*

Study the manual that is the universe, and know the fire that burns within. These instructions help us remove the obstructions. The deeper we dig, the more we study, the greater our discoveries.

What is the force that empowers the universe's immensity? What is the order in all the seeming chaos? What is holding it all together? Look into the world's book and ask: *Who wrote the instructions for this planet and others?*

Ask yourself: *Why is it that water is cool and fire hot?* Ask why some people

are cool and others hot. Ask why some places are cool and others hot.

To find the book of life, the instruction manual of how to live, we have to do two things: We have to zoom in and we have to zoom out.

Apply the same navigational tools you would for a digital map to the world's book: Zoom into focus on the tiniest details, explore their novelties, and then zoom out to see the bigger picture. Do this again and again, and again and again.

Flip through the pages of the world's book casually, then read them slowly, then highlight the sentences that stick out at you. And then read the book again, and again, and again.

It will then be, as you discover the world, that you will also come to discover your own true self.

And after that, as you begin to see your true self—your true image, your true fire—the world too will begin to see your true self, your true image, and your true fire.

Self-Imaging

After turning your eyes outward to the world, discovering that every nuance of creation instructs your fire and guides your prosperity, it is time to turn your eyes inward to your own self. How you see your very own self is the marrow of prosperity.

When you look at your own self you must appreciate that you have been formed in the image of an artist with the greatest self-image imaginable. Like the greatest piece of art, this image is indescribable, beyond words. The defiance of description, instead of detracting from the self-image, makes the self-image all the more profound.

If you see yourself as a fire, you will burn bright and true. If you see yourself as a mere collection of hard bone, decaying flesh, and congealing blood, you will live like a skeleton. Self-image is everything, because self-image allows you to see (or ignore) your true self and your deepest potential. Self-image is not foolish disillusionment; ignoring your fire is foolish disillusionment:

foolishly disillusioning yourself by thinking you are limited in your capacities.

You are only limited if you think you are limited. Do not, under any circumstances, think you are limited. Yes, you are a limited edition in that you are one-of-a-kind, but your uniqueness is unlimited.

A few decades ago, one could never imagine a cell phone, never mind today's smartphones; a few decades before that, no one could imagine a rocket ship. For most of human history, much of the world believed the world was flat. This all goes to show that the human being believes what it is trained to believe. A thousand years ago, prosperity was having a fast horse; today prosperity is buying a first-class ticket for a flight that can take you around the world in twenty-four hours. Who knows what prosperity holds in store for us tomorrow, or the day after, or throughout the rest of the future?

Do not limit your self-image and your image of the world. The future will come to bear your dreams.

Believe in your fire, in your own true self, in your essential light and warmth. Allow your self-image to be infinite, to be energetic and dynamic—to be anything and everything you can imagine, and then more.

The world's instructions were written just for you, to lift you higher, to increase your strength beyond the possible. We call it "inverse paranoia"— you are afraid of nothing, excited for everything. You just know that you are fire and everything around you is working for your favor.

Know and recognize that you are fire, and the world will know it too. Think that you are worthless and dispensable, and the world will think that as well. Possessing a righteous self-image is realizing and recognizing that your image is perfect.

This means that all you have to do is live up to your perfection.

Free Choice

The choice to (or not to) live up to your perfection is entirely and scarily up to you. Entirely because you are its sole practitioner; scarily because all things worthy give you goosebumps. But who was ever scared of scary? Your potential is scary, scary good. Acknowledge its awesome, earth-shattering power, and get on with it.

Prosperity is a choice. No. Incorrect. Prosperity is *the* choice, the choice to follow the instructions. Or not. A fire does not have a choice. It must burn and prosper. But to follow or to not follow the instructions—in how to apply the heat to all things and how to never stifle the fire—is the choice we must make.

Choice is one of our greatest blessings, but it can also be one of our greatest curses. When we choose wisely, it is our blessing. When we choose foolishly, it is our curse.

Today, more than at any other time in history, our choices are almost infinite in their variety and diversity. This open marketplace of ideas and ideologies could be liberating. It could also be paralyzing. Prosperity is when we choose to follow the fire and it is nonnegotiable. Prosperity is following the absolute.

Doubt is one of the greatest hindrances to the certainty of your fire. Allow the absolute truths that resonate within you to prosper and flourish. Do not stifle their growth by questioning their validity.

Why is it that when an athlete dedicates himself or herself to a certain sport with unwavering will and persevering determination, we applaud it; but when a human being wishes to do the same in her or his own personal life, we question the validity and doubt the certainty?

Because, in sports, success is very quantifiable: you win or you lose. Quantifying life, however, is impossible. And also because, at the end of the day, sports are inconsequential, and life is not.

Relativism believes that there are no absolute truths, that there are no empirical facts by which to guide your life.

Really? Is breathing optional? Is breathing relative to situation and circumstance? Try not breathing for a few minutes. You know what it is called? It is called asphyxiation. Is eating an absolute truth, or is eating optional relativism?

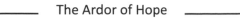
Just as (or maybe even more than) your body needs to eat, your fire needs to eat as well. It is not optional. Yes, some things are absolute, nonnegotiable, and eternal. You are absolute. Your fire is absolute. And, if you so choose, your prosperity will be absolute.

If you wish your prosperity to be optional, then it most certainly will be optional. Do not make such a rash decision. Or, if you do, change it fast.

Just as you make the healthy choice to breathe and the nourishing choice to eat, do the same for your fire. Allow your fire to breathe, feed your fire with the essential truth that you know and feel. Feed your prosperity and allow it to breathe. It is as absolute as nutrients and oxygen for your body.

If you do not question your body's absolute need to breathe and eat, do not question your soulful fire's absolute need to breathe and eat. This is how you will prosper.

It is your inalienable right to not feed your fire and to not allow your fire to breathe, just as it is your choice to not feed your body and not allow your lungs to inhale and exhale. But, being your right does not make it right. Such a choice is a choice, but it is a very unhealthy and catastrophic choice.

Our pursuit here is prosperity, not a daily grind of missed chances, anorexic thoughts, and emaciated lives. There is real happiness if you decide to follow the correct instructions. There are concrete, pointed, honed truths that bring you great abundance of joy. These instructions absolutely make you a very free person. This freedom is dependent solely on your free choice to choose freely.

Free choice is the ability to choose to be free. But free choice is also the ability to choose to be enslaved.

Do you wish to live in a self-constructed cell or in a self-liberating freedom?

Mentor Ship

Though there are no shortcuts to prosperity, there are some great tools that help ease the journey's burden, such as the aforementioned Instructions, World Book, and Self-Imaging. Another one of these tools is the Mentor.

Mentors are those seasoned veterans who have been there before, who have journeyed long and hard, and who have learned by experience what is healthy and what is not. One does not have to experience every up-and-down of life's terrain before discovering which instructions boost your fire's prosperity and which snuff it out.

Our first and most natural mentors are our parents. Parents have the ability to educate and instruct their children with such love and compassion that their children will grow up into secure and vibrant human beings— prospering fires that illuminate the world around them.

Parents also have the ability to do the opposite, to stifle and hinder a child's natural growth. When a mentor hurts and denigrates the flames entrusted into their care, doing the exact opposite of the mentor's very purpose, the mentor is perpetuating, terribly and painfully, the exact opposite of what the mentor is supposed to.

Our schoolteachers, religious and spiritual leaders, politicians, and role models are all mentors in a person's life. When such a position inspires and educates, it is beautiful; when it is corrupt and abusive, it is a sinful catastrophe.

It would be like a coach injuring an athlete; it would be like an engineer undermining a structure; it would be like a bitter wind blowing out an innocent candle—only worse. You see, we are talking here about the success and growth of a human life. If one cannot help it prosper, one had best move out of its way.

To be a mentor is a great responsibly. And so is seeking one out. Both mentorship and seeking a mentor must be performed with the perfect balance between humility and honesty.

Prosper One, Prosper All

A gross injustices to prosperity is applying it exclusively in a financial context. False prosperity prospers in one field, while all other fields decay. True prosperity is across all platforms and all mediums.

Do not confuse ones and zeroes with prosperity. Numbers are just numbers.

Prosperity is when all facets of your fire flourish. One form of prosperity is monetary, but your fire must prosper in your relationships, in your friendships, and in your kindness as well, not only in your business or work. If you only prosper monetarily but everything else in life is in steady decline, is that true prosperity? Is that real richness? If your bank accounts are rich but your heart is poor, is that true prosperity? If your wallet is brimming with cash but your ideals and principles are bankrupt, is that genuine prosperity?

Prosperity—true prosperity—occurs only when your fire is allowed to burn. And when you allow your fire to burn and apply its light and warmth to all aspects of living, then every element of your being, from your professional life to your personal life to your spiritual life, will prosper with this innate fire.

If you truly prosper in one thing, you will prosper in all. This is what a fire does. And if you falsely prosper in many things, you will prosper in none.

Begin by focusing on one aspect of your life in which you wish to prosper: for example, studying. Then study like a man possessed. Study as a fire burns: always adding, always increasing, and never stopping. In other words, study long and prosper!

Whichever specific item you make the focus of your flaming prosperity, approach it like walking into a vortex of invincibility, one that causes a shift in your life that brings the fire of your essence out in very tangible ways.

Bring your own uniqueness to the equation, and find yourself rising above the setbacks and disappointments you once thought were the norm.

As you focus on one specific aspect of your life, that prosperity will spill over into other aspects. Prosperity is contagious. Like a ball laboriously pushed up the hill, finally reaching the top, and beginning to gather momentum for the charge down. You begin to increase in every area of your life. And increase is the modus operandi of your fire, your soul.

Like a flickering flame, it aspires to burn higher and higher—never actually reaching the summit but every advance upward is a summit in its own right.

This is what a fire does. This is what your fire does.

Action Pact

As with all things deep and real, the words sometimes come easily but the true barometer is the actions they spawn.

Following the instructions of prosperity is one percent inspiration and ninety-nine percent actualization. A building is not built by drawing a blueprint. A building is built by implementing the blueprint's instructions.

The obstacles along the way are many, but if you remember the fire, you will never get sidetracked, and never cease building until the structure is manifested in the most complete, tangible, and prosperous way.

This is the blueprint. It is now time to implement.

~~

More than an answer,
Prosperity is a calling.

CHAPTER THREE

Matter & Spirit

Matter is the bulb; spirit the light.
Matter is the barrel; spirit the wine.
Matter is the canvas; spirit the art.

~~

Knowledgeable Power

Power is a fascinating word. Throughout the history of the world, power was associated with physical strength. The bigger someone was, the taller someone stood, or the better someone battled, the more powerful that someone was. With the advancements of technology, and the mass dissemination of information, we have come to realize that, in many ways, knowledge is the most powerful force in existence, more so than brute force or physical muscle. Indeed, the well-known aphorism, attributed to Sir Francis Bacon, says this fact in three simple words: "Knowledge is power."

Knowledge comes in many shapes and sizes. Logic would dictate that the power is directly related to the knowledge: The greater the knowledge, the greater the power; and the more profound the knowledge, the more profound the power. If, after all, knowing itself were powerful, then holding the most important knowledge would seem to be the most powerful.

For example: knowing that fire is hot is powerful; but how much more powerful is knowing *why* fire is hot, or *how* to utilize that heat?

What, then, is the single most powerful piece of information one can possess? If you had one thing—one thing alone—to impart to your children, what would that piece of knowledge be? What is the primary knowledge to know?

If one were a flame, a fire burning—and, as we have come to learn, every individual is one such flame—what is the single most important piece of information that would fuel one's fire to burn bright and true?

What capsule of knowledge will ensure that your fire burn as powerful and wonderful as possible?

The Foundation

Please pause reading for a moment and look at the world around you. Yes, please pause for a moment and look at the world around you. Do you see the heavens above and the earth below? Do you see the sun setting and the tides rising? Do you see the trees rustling and the birds soaring? Do you see the stars twinkling and the clouds floating?

From where do these phenomena come? Do you know who made them? Did you perhaps fashion them yourself? Or perchance it was your neighbor?

Now look within, into your own self. Do you feel your heart beating and your mind churning? Do you see your fingers flicking and your eyes flickering? Do you hear your mouth speaking and your blood pumping?

From where does all of this come? Who formed you into being? Did you perhaps do so yourself? Or was it your parents? Perhaps you are the summation of highly sophisticated matter? Or, maybe you are constantly imbued with an indelible spirit? What is the foundation of existence?

Electricity illuminates a light bulb; what illuminates you? What injects life into the living?

The foundation of all foundations, and the pillar of all wisdom, is to know that neither you, nor any other human being, nor any other creature, created this material world. No matter, no matter how large or small, created the matter that constitutes the universe we know and love. Biology did not create biology and matter did not create matter. Creations do not create; creations are created. As you look (and even as you do not) at the countless layers of existence—more vast than any human mind could ever comprehend—the foundation of all knowledge is to know that the matter you see is but a result of a creative force, the force of existence: the force of existence itself.

You and I have the ability to transform this matter into breathtaking beauty. You and I have the power to whip this matter up into frothy delights. But you and I do not have the power to create this matter from scratch.

This is the single most important piece of knowledge one can obtain, and this is the source of our greatest power: To know that there is a Primary Being—a Prime Essence that made, and continues to make, something from nothing, that makes matter from no matter, and that makes all things from no things—is to know the very soul of existence itself.

And, once one knows the very soul of existence, one can begin connecting to the soul of existence.

Within every particle and subatomic particle, and within every molecule and nucleus of matter, there is a spirit that drives it and makes it be. This spirit is the energy and power emanating from and sourced in the Prime Being of existence.

After all matter is created, only then do we creations have the ability to utilize that matter to form other matter; to fashion products and produce fashions; to shape creation and create shapes from shaped creation. We are chefs in a kitchen pantry stocked with the most sublime ingredients. But we did not create the ingredients; we merely employ their gifts to create sublime dishes from them, to the best of our abilities.

There is a spirit that empowers and creates all matter. This knowledge is the greatest power that one can possess. And this possession is the greatest gift that one can know.

Only after recognizing that spirit creates and empowers matter, can we have the divine ability to dig deep into the matter and mine from its origins and depths the spirit of all things.

First and Last

This piece of knowledge is more important than all others because it establishes what is primary to life and living, and distinguishes it from what is but secondary—what is essential and what is optional, what comes first and what comes last, what is the main course and what is but an appetizer, what is merely the wooden cask and what is the divine wine, what is living and what is skeletal.

This is important for the same reason it is important to differentiate between a musical instrument and music itself.

An instrument is made of very unmusical matter, like wood or brass. A musical instrument, say a violin, is not music in and of itself. Music itself resides within the musician. When it itches for release, the musician picks up the violin and, by drawing the bow across the mundane strings, the unmusical instrument unleashes the musician's inner music.

This great universe is a musical composition, composed by the Cosmic Composer. The countless manifestations of matter we feel and touch are the instruments, unmusical and mundane in their own right. But through these instruments of matter the inner music is released and realized. The inner music itself is the spirit; the instrument is the matter. The primary knowledge allows us to differentiate between the material instruments of existence and the spiritual music. And this knowledge is our power.

Thinking that matter is the source of matter and creates matter is like thinking a violin is the source of music and creates musicians. It is the artist who creates musical instruments so that music lives and breathes, not the other way around. Have you ever seen a violin create music as it lies there in its case? It is impossible. Only once the musician picks up the material violin and begins to play it, does the music commence its flow.

If this is the case with simple music, how much more true is it with a complex universe! Nothing—absolutely not one thing—can live without being alive. No matter can exist without the spirit playing its songs.

An innocent child looks at a violin and thinks the violin itself creates music. Then the child grows up, matures, and acquires the correct knowledge, and begins to know and see that the musician but uses the violin as a tool by which to produce his or her inner music. A neophyte looks at the world and thinks matter creates the symphony of existence. When the neophyte grows up, he or she gains an understanding that matter is but the instruments through which the Cosmic Composer chooses to play the symphonic melodies of life and being.

Without this knowledge, one may think that biological matter and physical material is the source of all life and the creator of all things. Knowing that there is a Primary Composer—a source for all the world's music—allows us to compose static matter into dynamic symphonies. Literally and musically.

Rocky Waters

Can I turn rock into water? Can I turn matter into spirit?

Have you ever seen the hurtling waves crash against the firm rocks? Water and rock seem to contradict one another: water is fluid and in motion; rock is solid and stationary.

Like the difference between the musical instrument and music itself, water and rock are excellent metaphors for spirit and matter: water is spirit, and rock matter.

Rock is static, water dynamic. Rocks are heavy, burdensome, hard, and unforgiving. Looking at a rock you do not see life. Water, on the other hand, is alive and feeds life. Water runs and makes things grow. Fish are at home in water; water quenches your thirst.

Matter is comatose, like rock; spirit is dynamic, like water, conducive to life and energizing all.

Sometimes you look at other people and they seem to be rocks. Sometimes

you look at your own self and you think you are a rock, comatose and inanimate. But remember the source of the rock and you will remember the water. Remember the music and the violin itself will come to life.

This, my fellow Fires, is how we turn rock into water. This is how we turn matter into spirit.

As intelligent beings, knowing that spirit transcends all matter engenders a consciousness that all things work together for the good—and herein is its power. Just as performing a musical composition connects and harmonizes the many instruments in an orchestra, so does the greater spirit connect and harmonize the many instruments of matter in this universal orchestra.

Once one knows that there is a spirit and energy within all of matter—a musical current of life that pulses through all of existence—how could one not turn rock into water? The rock's very core *is* water.

When we have this knowledge, and wrap our minds around it, our mind's eye can peer through this lens of clarity and see the world as it truly is: a material instrument of living music. This brings profound hopefulness even in the harshest of times. Knowing that within the darkest rock lives a fresh spring of well water, that even within the coldest matter flickers a spark and spirit that energizes it, is powerful enough to invigorate and humble you.

The only challenge—and it is a challenge—is to see and uncover it. But uncovering the inner spirit results in an eruption from within the dense rock. Yesterday it seemed to be improbable, if not downright impossible, to see a water source within this earthbound rock. But today, our knowledge allows us to see the inner water as it gushes forth in an unstoppable flow.

One must always seek and see the lesson in all things created and in all circumstances formed. One must always look deeper than the instrument, into the very music itself. Behind these rocks, which we perceive as barren and invincible, lies the power to release a good, sweet, thirst-quenching spring of water, hydrating the parched soul.

Despair is thinking a hard rock is only a hard rock; or thinking an instrument has no potential for music. This is a deceptive untruth. Without the knowledge that there is a Prime Source for all matter and that all matter is preceded by spirit, one may conclude that turning a stagnant rock into flowing water would be impossible. But once one downloads the fact that all is created by a Prime Spirit and within all does this spirit live, then one recognizes the fictitious façade of rock for what it really is: the flow of divine water dressed in a mineral costume.

The Fine Infinite

Our minds are finite. Existence is infinite. Instruments are finite. Music is infinite. Matter is finite. Spirit is infinite. Without the knowledge of what is what, our finite minds may project their finite perceptions unto creation and into matter. But once we know that the Infinite Reality precedes and creates finite existence, then this infinite universal truth triumphs over the finite world.

If matter itself—that which we can see—is so substantial, imagine the vast substantiality of the things we cannot see. If one solitary violin represents and embodies beautiful music, just imagine how much more beautiful the music is in its essential state—unfathomably beautiful, beautifully unfathomable!

The so-called "reality" that gestates in our thoughts, is rarely the end product. Events are rarely predictable. Often you may think that you are powerless to overcome a certain obstacle. The spirit you received is infinitely greater than any matter. And this is an understatement. And even that was an understatement.

When two rocks come together they clash; when two bodies of water come together they conjoin and flow as one harmonious body of water. When two musical instruments are bashed together, they crash and bang and clash; but when two notes of pure music come together, they harmonize and synthesize. When an element of matter meets another element of matter, the two elements clash; but when two elements of spirit meet, they fuse and unite as one.

This is the fundamental difference between the finite and the infinite: The former only allows for limited perspectives and limited capacities; while the latter sees only unlimited possibilities.

The origin for this is the foundation of all foundations, that the Primary

Mover and Shaker is limitless and unified in Its source. The spirit and life-source of everything contains the ability to transform everything, and, on a prime level, everything It creates has, at its essence, a limitless and unified element as well.

Transformers

Matter looks a certain way; it has a definitive texture and feel to. By digging deeper and revealing its innate spirit we can transform it into something else, something more. We may not have the ability to create matter, but, by the power vested in us, we do have the ability to create change and transform matter.

By engaging the potent instructions and studying the guiding principles, one begins to actively bond with the flame in addition to the wick. It resonates within one's deepest soul and the spirit leaps forth, penetrating into the atomic fabric of the world, metamorphosing forms and functions. It is the essence of matter starting to matter. What was once thought of as a matter of inconceivable belief becomes, as a matter of fact, a joyous material reality.

You see that person you once knew—and that person might very well be yourself—who once seemed to be as interesting as a rock, and about as alive. And now, poof: The person's very core evolved into a whole new being, one that is surrounded by an ever-present light, shining righteously, righteously bright, brightly inspiring, inspiringly sprite.

What happened? What changed? Something very simple happened: The matter yielded to the spirit, the instrument yielded to the music, and the person yielded to the right instructions, becoming its product. This righteousness can only be accomplished with the vim and vigor of spirit.

Before, you were looking at matter with material eyes; now you look at the world with spiritual eyes. By focusing your attention upon a bigger picture than the one painted by your own circumstances, even the tiniest pixels come to life and the entire picture changes. You still look up from this material plane, but, suddenly, now you look up with spiritual eyes and through a spirited prism, one for whom despair disappears and depression holds no impression.

This is absolute. Some may call it truth. Some may not call it at all. The tangible matter upon which, at this very moment, you stand is, in essence, a canvas of and for spirit. This resonates within each and every man, woman, and child. Our all-encompassing, all-consuming fires contain a measure of innate faith that can never be extinguished. Period. The accumulation of all these beliefs directs your path. Believe it, trust it, activate it, and allow the spiritual hope in all tangible matter to flow. Resultantly, all fires will be triumphant and every spirit will triumph.

Musical Genius

Meet an accomplished musician. A righteous gracefulness and sublime aura permeates the musician's being: a oneness, born of the knowledge that, even without a witness to the music performed, the musician has transcended the matter of this world and entered into a spiritual realm. The musical genius takes what, at first glance, seems to be beyond possible, and turns it into a symphonic chorus, synthesizing and harmonizing all things. It leaves us breathless, awed, and humbled.

We get this sense of breathlessness whenever we come in contact with the people who tap into their inner spirit by ardently pursuing an endeavor with all their mind, soul, heart, and spirit. This is what we call beauty, art, genius, and it soars for all of humanity to gloriously behold. These artists, conjurers, and dreamers elevate their pursuits to a spiritual plane by conquering and transcending the plain of the material.

We are all geniuses and we are all musicians, each of us playing divine melodies. Whether one is a teacher, carpenter, or engineer; whether one is retired, laid-off, or a workaholic, each and every one of us has a sublime song we can—and must—share with the world. This is called finding the spirit within the matter, the water within the rock, the music that is your soul within the instrument that is your body.

This is called getting in touch with your all-consuming Fire. And letting it burn.

This is called musical genius. Each one of us is a musical genius. The only question is: What type of music do we play and how often do we yield to our genius?

The Results

Knowing the timelessness of spirit strengthens you at all times. As with any machine, it helps to know how it works. It works like this: In your own strength, founded upon the knowledgeable power, you become weary, faint of heart, parched and yearning. You begin to thirst less for the rock and more for the wellspring of water. This thirst causes the living waters to pour openly into the cistern of this known world. So vastly does it pour that all the vessels in the world and all the instruments of matter could never hold its deluge. This spirit runs over all containment and parameters. It runs and spills over into others and they desire to drink from this fountain as well. They want this water that conquers their life's thirst. Everyone feels empty wanting fulfillment that only the spiritual can give.

The first step to implementation is knowing that this core spirit of yours is stronger and more powerful than any alloy of matter known to man. After this first step, your might can overcome any and all circumstances that are created by humankind. While your instruments and circumstances may be limited and finite, your substance is not.

Your essence is not mediocre and you therefore cannot live in mediocrity. You cannot restrict the love you possess. Know that the love generator that lives within you is by far greater than anything in the world outside of you. Always activate this love, this fire, which connects you to the spiritual self.

The resounding fact is you are not merely a competing being for—nor an object of—the material realm. Sure, you live in a material world, but a material world does not live in you. You are a spiritual being and it is your calling to know the spirit of all things.

One may pursue one of two things: one may pursue matter, or one may pursue spirit. Food, clothing, and housing, are material things. They are musical instruments. Purposefulness, soulfulness, and kindness are spiritual things. They are the music.

When you pursue spirit, matter follows; but when you pursue matter, spirit flees. The spirit delivers all to you simply and naturally. Suddenly, no longer is there a conscious effort to attain more matter; it is just there, that's it, simply there: no struggles, no seeking money or merits, to attain such things. Rather, it is like the musician who dazzles effortlessly.

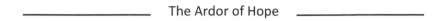
Sure, we have two voices, one cold and rough, the other sweet and warm:

The darkness may say, the rock may say, the inanimate object that is matter may say: My marriage is broken; my son is lost; I have a physical illness that the 'experts' say is incurable, they say I must yield to it and get my affairs in order because I have little time left in the world, they say death is here.

But this is only matter speaking, cold and rough. Now enter spirit.

Spirit says: Oh, but let the fire in you rise up, light up, and sing up: Allow the physical reality to begin dissolving in your mind's eye. This reality that you shaped in your mind's eye is but holding you back from the real you. Start believing that what is within you is greater than what is outside of you. You came ex nihilo into this material world. Why don't you just start believing today that what was formed came from what wasn't formed? And then you can know that this spirit can alter everything. So rise up with great knowledge of the truth that, yes, someday my body may return to dust, but the spirit that created me—the light that lives inside of me—is greater than anything in this material realm.

Every single human being, from the greatest sage to the simplest novice, carries this gentle voice of spirit. You were formed with this from the beginning. It penetrates the intellect and permutes the course of thought, allowing you to recognize that you can triumph over all things.

Remember where we started: the Fire, the Consuming Fire. This fire that consumes all matter is from this spirit. You direct this with the knowledge you possess, and the result is a rock gushing forth with transformative wellsprings of water. From the Fire's instructions, your obedience has followed.

This is the trajectory: First you recognize your Consuming Fire, then you follow its instructions, and finally it results in all the rocks of matter turning into waters of spirit.

Matter of Fact

One's hard work, diligence, and nuanced planning do not guarantee success. Many people turn over their lives, transform their work, and still live in mediocrity, frustrated daily and blinded by depression. Joy, like a silent guest, comes every day, every morning, every moment, no matter the circumstance—yet, it is recognized only when we look past a world formed of material and into an existence created by the spiritual. All our work and plans and accomplishments are mere media whose success is contingent on the ignition, cognition, and recognition of something more.

Our success is contingent on our spirit, but our spirit is not contingent on our success.

We reside in the world of emotions cycling through the spheres of our own bodies. These emotions convey our motions and moods from within our inner selves, and they propel us. Truly understanding life as a test, challenging us to overcome any obstacle that is put in front of us, gives us a confidence to get into the solution-finding mindset, inspiring us to feed from the spiritual realm that the eternal sages and timeless mystics have spoken of through the ages and pages.

Understanding that our physical gifts and material capacities are analogous to a musical instrument, places the onus upon us to learn how to play the instrument like a virtuoso. The result is an unstoppable waterfall of music, a wellspring that floods adversity with such goodness that you live a joyful life, never depending on the matter of the material but using it to propel you forward by trusting wholeheartedly that the good always triumphs over the opposite.

Ash and decay fade with time; light and sparks increase. So you see the adversity, you feel the despair, and a spirit of depressing anxiety moves over you. Well, if you accept that depression and anxiety and darkness are real, why can you not accept that joy and pleasure and light are just as real? You— yes, you!—have the power to choose what source you want to draw from: from a well of good or a well of the opposite. Because there is a spiritual warfare that you can choose sides on, and because of the fact that history has written proof that the spring of well-water of good always triumphs.

So let go of that spiritual depression, the existential despair that grips you, trying to wrestle every bit of life force out of you. It wants you to look down at the downsides, and even upsides, of your life. Look up, instead, and see the upside of your life, and turn even the downsides up. You have been given this gift. It is not by determinism. We do not determine what in life is rock and what is water. That has been determined by the Prime Creator of all rock and water. But with the knowledge gifted to us, we do have the power to determine whether we wish to follow the rocks in life or life's waters, whether we wish to know only the comatose instruments or to tap into the oscillating music itself.

When we use our primary knowledge to choose wisely, we have the power to turn even rock itself into water. By your own strength shall you then turbocharge your journey through this life. By recognizing that outside, as well as inside, of your own true self—indeed, in everything you see, and in every creature you know—an awesome inspiring spiritual realm is there to connect with and thrust you above any and all darkness to a light of real joy.

To connect to this abundant joy that is sustainable through any and all circumstances, your intellect must have faith that the spiritual will triumph over matter. To generate such power is to engage in the will of love that all mankind possesses. Hold out for the very best in your life. Refuse to submit to anything else but the very best that you aspire to be. Doubt will definitely try to subdue you in bonds of despair—the opposite of the outcome you desire. The spirit in you gives you the ability and inclination to act to accept the good will to overcome, no matter the matter. So stop that decaying way of thinking, of obsessing over imaginary fears and anxieties. Quit it, outwit it; it will never serve you.

Our goal is a full generation and complete regeneration of spirit, goodness, and dynamic water. Anything less is nothing at all.

Harmony

Harmony is not what happens when you have only spirit; when you have matter and spirit, harmony is what happens when they fuse.

Imagine a picture of the best of you. This will harmonize all emotions. This will harmonize all events and circumstances. The ultimate knowledge is powerful, but it still only remains knowledge. Harmonization allows that knowledge to implement in a manifested and tangible way throughout all facets of your existence, in addition to your intellect. What you think with your intellect is only the beginning; harmony in music allows all the different elements—musicians, notes, scales, articulations, tones, composers, arrangers, conductors, instruments—to sequentially gather and coalesce within this one soldering and smoldering spirit. Know that the spiritual guidance is a connection to the agreement of all your purposes. Know that the spirit creates this abundant joy, overcoming any dissonance that comes between you and your mission to build a better place for all to dwell in.

The connection of souls to this harmonized good comes through spiritual means. Our power is finite; the spiritual is infinitely good in all things. The real joy is the binding of love to those around you, attracting people that harmonize with your higher self on this material plane. We can all analyze, time and time again, and ruminate until our heads are dizzy. However, the matter that manifests in this revealed world is created in another world that is concealed to our clothed and material eyes. This unseen world is by far greater than the revealed world. Its power is so awesome that it bends, moves, and subdues this known universe. This spiritual realm is all-encompassing, all-powerful, and awe-inspiring. This spiritual realm resides within you, walks with you, oversees you, guides you, lives in you, and loves you.

It only asks that you return the favor. All it asks is for you to reside within it: for you to walk with it, oversee it, guide it, live in it, and love it.

It would be a gross misunderstanding to think that harmony removes all distinction. The individuality of each of the sounds that make up a harmony must remain distinct, and without those specific pitches and tone colors, there is no harmony at all. But also, harmony happens only when one can differentiate between matter and spirit. Harmonious music can only be created when the musician can define what is instrument and what is music. Thinking music is instrument and instrument is music will result in noisy dissonance, causing earsplitting headaches.

Learn to appreciate the difference between what is spiritual and what is matter. Discontent, anxiety, and doubt are outgrowths of not recognizing the difference between matter and spirit, and they are the results of being unaware that each works in a unique way. Trying to feed spirit with matter would be as detrimental as trying to expect matter to be as inspiring as spirit. Without distinction, one may start thinking: *You know, I just wish I had that new car; I wish I had that house; man, look at that person; boy, that would make me so happy.* Get ahold of yourself. Realize that all good things will come when you know that in harmonizing with your matter and spirit, your

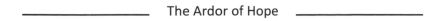

goodness and love of both self and other will permeate and vitalize and revitalize.

Remember the powerful knowledge that spirit precedes and creates matter, and recognize that it is impossible to fill a spiritual void with items of matter. A new car will not rev the engine of your soul, nor quench its thirst.

You may not be the world's greatest at one thing, but you certainly are at something else. This is why you were created: for an assignment that's greater than you. This transcends all matter because you are spiritually led. Please seek wise counsel. Seek the right path. Allow this to seep deep into your subconscious, which will direct the flow of all the good you desire. Also allow this to seep deep into your conscious state. Always stay open and willing to seek advice. Don't be hardheaded and stubborn. Create the boldness in you to make the correct decisions.

This isn't to hurt anyone's feelings or to run over anyone. You just don't want to run in circles for life's assignment. As a matter of fact, this will inspire and elevate the people around you as well. Be the person you were made to be, not seeking approval from everyone else. Once you realize the spiritual, you will live without the guilt and without the abandonment; you will conquer the pull to be like others, and instead you will be the original you.

This spiritual connection will take you places you never dreamed before. It will take you higher than you ever imagined. The flow and ease with which you live is incomprehensible to the known world. You will be alien to them all, but deeply connected to all beings. Triumph is yours over all the setbacks and put-downs. A war is raging around you to get your attention.

Why wrestle with it? Allow the master to teach, allow the electricity to electrify, allow the spirit to spiritualize your soul, allow your music to resound, and allow the spark to ignite your fire.

The spirit indwells in all things. The realm of this spirit is the sphere and atmosphere of one's life. Such a life transacts its business in the spiritual realm. Your life in this material world needs more than human power. Yes, we all can agree that the human energy of the will, heart, and mind will achieve awesome human results. But this natural world limits us. The supernatural is the magical kingdom we aspire to.

Matter and spirit exist. This is beyond our control. It is up to us to ensure that they always complement one another and never contradict.

Earth Boundless

As we grow, submitting to and trusting in this spiritual realm, sometimes we are blinded by the ignorance of our own minds. We think that we are earthbound, bound by and to material longitude, attitude, and altitude. You must allow the clear conviction to permeate your being. Say it: I am not earthbound! I am not earthbound! I am earth boundless! I am bounded by no matter, but freed by all spirit. And by being bound to nothing I can bond with everything.

Make no mistake about it; there are dark forces in this universe, forces that try to tie us down, to destroy the spiritual good to which we aspire. Like a trained athlete, or a honed soldier, we must practice every day to acclimate ourselves to this spiritual side. Belief alone is not enough. It is a starting point but not an ending point, not when we are in a constant battle with dark winds.

Certainly, it is much easier to seek provisions, or distractions, or anything really, than to deal with the stubbornness of the human heart. But the only thing that can bind you to earth is your own self—and this means you and you alone possess the key to unlock this door. Perpetual practice, refining, honing, and training ensures that this will be so. There will never be a contradiction. Your free will shall reveal the differences in the spiritual and the material—and the harmony in these differences. You will influence all things with the practice of using your material faculties to know the spiritual realities—and your spiritual realities to know the true sublime essence of the material faculties.

Then, the seemingly limited capacity of the rock expands into the unlimited flow of the water; the simple instrument of wood and glue projects and amplifies the most profound music of ethereal proportions.

This is how you fashion the material earth into a magnificent garden of spirit and paradise, a paradise on earth for all to inhabit.

Knowing this most powerful knowledge will give you the authority to speak over all matter.

And all matter shall listen.

This will give you the confidence to pick up your material instrument and play your spiritual music.

And, if you listen carefully, you can hear the entire universe as it sings along.

~~

For nature to proceed
and matter to succeed,
spirit must precede.

CHAPTER FOUR

Intellect

What you put in your mouth shapes your hips.
What you put in your mind shapes you.

~~

Intellectual Property

We have thus far been dabbling in fire. It is high time we started to burn.

It is one thing to have a fire burn inside of you; it is quite another for that fire to take over your entire being, to infuse all your thoughts, feelings, and actions with its light. It is one thing to strive for prosperity; it is quite another for the prosperity to be real and equitable. It is one thing to want to turn matter into spirit, to desire for rock to become water; it is quite another for the stony expressionless matter to actually be turned into the vibrant waters of spirit.

It is quite a big leap from inspiration to reality, as is the leap from theory to fact. Inspiration is necessary, but it is not enough. Inspiration must lead to action. And action begins with intellect.

The Pilot

If the fire fuels the engine of your vehicle, then the intellect is your pilot. Like a pilot, the intellect directs your entire being and navigates the roads of life. Acquiring a good handle on your pilot, on your intellect, is essential to acquiring a good handle on your life.

The first step, then, in actualizing your inner fire, realizing your prosperity, and turning your matter into spirit is to master your intellect and become intimate with the piloting force that it is.

The human being is structured in a very precise, intricate, and detailed manner. While positioned upright, an individual stands head over heart, and heart over legs. As the human is shaped, so does the human go. The head, the brain, the mind controls and pilots the heart, legs, and collective body.

To implement the fire of your soul throughout the rises and dips of the body's contours, it would be wise to begin by grabbing hold of and maintaining your grasp on your mind and intellect.

Focusing your mind—never mind changing it—is easier said than done, especially after years of habitual action and programmed routines. Intellects are tricky things; they are immensely powerful and very difficult to master. Informing the innocent mind of a child, say, is relatively straightforward, like writing with fresh ink on new parchment. But informing the jaded mind of an adult is quite difficult, like writing with old ink on repurposed, recycled, reconditioned parchment. How then do you change and influence your overprogrammed mind?

Perhaps, instead of changing your mind itself, it would be best to change the content that enters your mind. If you were to become the curator of your mind's content, you would also cure and curate your mind's intellect— and if you curate your intellect—your pilot—then you also curate your entire body and its movements.

Okay, content it is. But wait: What exactly is 'content'? How can we acquire it? How do we discover it? What does it look like?

Automobile

Feel the wind as you open her up on a coastal highway. The rev of the engine and the vroom of its life are almost human. As the automobile moves along the blacktop, likewise the human being moves along the road of life. The automobile is an apt metaphor for the human being as it journeys through the highways and byways of existence.

In the automobile industry, the word 'content' refers to everything the car has. Content does not refer to the car itself, to the car body, the car skeleton, the car-type or manufacturer. Rather, content refers to what the car possesses. For instance, content may refer to the car's air conditioning, power windows, leather seats, power door locks, twenty-two-inch wheels, or navigation system. Content is the product we superimpose upon the car's basic framework, by means of choice, will, and preference.

Applying this metaphor to the human being allows us to differentiate between the intellectual mind itself, and that mind's superimposed content. The mind is comparable to the car's skeletal makeup; the content is all the features the mind possesses. The information you feed your brain is like the content attached to the basic car body.

This distinction is essential. Why? Because though we may not necessarily control the potentials and limits of our mind—after all, do we choose our brains any more than we do our birth?—we certainly do control what content goes into, and is best suited for, our minds.

The importance of controlling your mind's content has everything to do with the mechanisms of your bodyworks.

In an overly generalized summation, you are structured as follows: Your intellect codes your thoughts; your thoughts create your emotions; and your emotions determine your actions. But what informs your intellect to code your thoughts? Your intellect requires information, content, and ideas to process. This is the content you feed your intellectual mind.

As with an automobile, there are superb car bodies with mediocre content;

just as there are mediocre car bodies with superb content. There are superb intellects with mediocre content, just as there are mediocre intellects with superb content. You are born with your intellect and your brain; but you acquire your content.

How smart you are is not the content. Much of humankind has vast intellectual capacity, but many humans are often filled with unexceptional content. Someone with an average intellect might possess brilliant content, while someone with a brilliant intellect might possess average content.

The key to any successful journey is to allow the right content into your mind, while sifting out the wrong; to acquire the best possible content and to open up the self to the infinite possibilities that surpass our very finite skeletons. Yes, our content can be unlimited in nature and scope, even though our brain apparatus may not be. This is not unlike the finite pen instrument composing the most infinitely sublime poetry.

Thus, the question you must ask yourself is this: What content does my intellect possess? What unique features—what windows to the world, what steering wheels of navigation, what power brakes to slow down, and what air conditioning to cool off—does your brain possess?

Most of us, most of the time, are fed mediocre content—which is really more con than content. The television shows we watch and the websites we visit generally convey mind-numbing content at best, and mind-scarring content at worst. Very little, if any, of the content we digest relates to our essential fires and burning flames; most of it is the coal of life, not its blaze.

The key to realizing your fire is to search for and connect with fiery content. If an automobile desires to navigate unknown territory, a GPS is essential. If an automobile wishes to take tight, sharp turns, a great steering apparatus and superior chassis and suspension system would be most beneficial. So too our intellects: To navigate the roads of life, which are often bumpy and full of bumper-to-bumper traffic, the correct content is paramount.

Providing the correct content to your mind drives your journey to be ridiculously luxurious. In an automobile you wouldn't switch out a steering wheel for a cartwheel, would you? You wouldn't replace your headlights with floodlights. In an automobile, the correct content is essential and no sane person would replace the appropriate content with the inappropriate.

How much more so with your own mind and intellect? For the journey of life to be as pleasurable, luxurious, and smooth as possible, the correct content is key.

Import Export

If the right content is important in a temporal thing such as an automobile, how much more important is it with an essential thing, such as our minds and intellects?

With a vehicle, one would never think of replacing the power brakes with powerless brakes. Why? Because powerless brakes inevitably result in head-on collisions, and no one desires a collision. With regard to an automobile, the consequences and ramifications of the correct or incorrect content are stark and clear.

With a human being, however, it's not so simple. So many different sources of content stream into the human mind constantly, making it difficult to sift through it all, retaining only the cream and discarding the rest of the crop.

With the incorrect content—flawed brakes—the human can crash, with ramifications more subtle but no less devastating than an automobile crash. But the human is unsure, flooded by countless options: One can farm one's mind with content from the web, television, or movies; from books, scholars, pundits, or polemical preachers; one can listen to pop music, go to universities, or simply look out of a bedroom window for ready-made content. Indeed, everything you experience, consciously or not, is content. Your intellect processes it all, and all of it shapes you.

We don't choose whether we consume content; once we're exposed to it, we've processed it to an extent. We only choose which content to willfully acquire and consume.

Another complexity is that the mind is exceptionally skilled at positing convincing arguments for detrimental content. The mind is an expert at justification. Your intellect is powerful and it can easily convince you that mediocre content is really what you need.

It is not. Mediocre content is what you do not need. You are alive, ablaze,

afire—and a fire needs conflagrating, inspiring, illuminating content to make it burn. Anything less would be like throwing dirt on a flame or a shackle on a dream. Anything less will not do. Anything less will depress, compress, or suppress your fire. It is our desire to express, impress, and stress our fire.

And in this, the correct content is king.

Freeing Will

Content, then, is subject to our will. Just as we and we alone choose which foods to put into our mouths, we and we alone choose what content to put into our heads.

As with an automobile, it is quite difficult to alter the basic car body itself, but it is relatively simple to modify the content that goes into the car body and attaches to its skeleton. This is true with your vehicle as well: It is quite difficult to change the actual structure, wiring, and body of your mind, but it is relatively simple to modify the content that goes into your mind, which informs your principles, decision-making, and actions.

Once your intellect acquires the right content, the right emotions will ensue, followed by the right action.

Your body is a cyclic machine; your Free Will informs this cycle and oils its gears. You do not choose to breathe or think—but you do choose *what* to breathe and think.

As your body moves in a rhythmic cycle, so does your experiential living. The mind informs action, and action changes the mind. This, of course, works both ways: The content you choose to consume informs your intellect, which creates emotions, which inspires actions. And then your experienced actions and emotions create new memories, new intellectual patterns and, as it were, new content upon which to restart the cycle. Or start a new one.

Consequently, by merely changing one cog in the sublime cycle that is you— the cog being the content—you actually change yourself!

Your will controls your discipline, allowing you to restrain the impulses and antics of troubling content. Your will builds your faith—faith in your own self and in the Creator of all self. Your will also lays the bedrock of your focused limitations and necessary barriers, essential elements in the specifications and specialization of life. Put another way: All of the world's content is none of the world's content—Free Will allows you to categorize and define and differentiate.

As mentioned, everything in life provides content. When you walk down the street or sit in a restaurant, or even when you sleep, you are downloading and processing content. It is your choice, and your choice alone, which content to embrace and which to ignore, which to internalize and which to extract, which to live by and which to bye-bye.

Animal Farm

This, my dear spark, is the difference between you and an animal. An animal's assignment has been coded into the animal's being. Animals have preprogrammed content and cannot change it, for better or worse. Nor do they desire to. This is why animals will never torture other animals or abuse their own children. But this is also why an animal will never discover a cure for illness or inspire a broken man to toss his brokenness aside.

Animals are what they are. But human beings are what they can become.

We have the ability to change our content, upgrade it, better it, enhance it, and transform it. More than ability, this in fact is the very thing that defines us as human beings: Our power to change, innovate, and become.

Indeed, the saddest thing would be for someone to believe that the content one has is final and unchangeable. Animals do, not human beings. If a simple automobile's content can change with a few turns of a screwdriver, or if a temporal smartphone's content can change with a basic software upgrade, how much more can the human mind update, adapt, and upgrade the content that enters its mind and informs its emotions and actions. Yes, it is much more work than a mere twist of a screwdriver or downloading an app, but that's only because it is much more profound.

Have you ever asked yourself: *Why do I desire to be more, to be better, to reach higher? Why do I always look for a source for all things? Why do I wish to connect with something beyond and everything around? Why do I always want to learn more, know more, understand more? Why do I have to transcend? Why am I afraid to be earthbound? Why can I not just simply live?*

The answer lies not in your intellect, not in your mind, nor even in your content.

Absent Mind

Though you do mind your thoughts, you are not mind. Meaning: You use your mind; your mind does not use you. Though you desire content—even create it—content does not create you. There is more to you than meets the mind. The mind is but your fire's hard drive and processing system. The mind is your most sophisticated tool, but it is still a tool. You are a fire and your intellect is a tool that helps your fire burn.

There is a fundamental question that a mind attempts to answer; there is an elemental thirst that the mind attempts to quench. But the mind is not the thirst. The mind is not the question. The fire is. A healthy intellect is one that focuses its resources on answering your fire's calling. A confused intellect is one that thinks it is the calling, and the answer. This is why success can still leave one sad, empty, and depressed. Material success may provide all sorts of content, but does the content address and feed the fire?

The fundamental stress placed on content is immense. Why? Because the very fire that drives our being—indeed, *is* our being—must understand the meaning of all things. And we understand by acquiring the right content.

To this end, we spend—or take on debt of—tens of thousands of dollars on education: hundreds of hours on the web; seminars and classes on everything and anything. We download and acquire content we think we need—ways to make money, secrets to dating, methods of cooking, forms of style, and on and on.

What is the source of this? Sure, monetary drive is big; desire for power is huge; but essentially we desire to master life and conquer its purpose. These are the dreams of success that drive the chase.

Yet, one can win an Oscar, a Super Bowl, a Most Valuable Player award, a

Nobel Prize, or a Presidency, and still possess an unrest, an uncertainty, a void in their existence, or a lack of soul peace.

The wrong content says: This is because you do not have enough of these things; you need more; you have to buy more; you need more power, more money, more options.

But, this at best is coming from your own mind with your own subjective agenda—and at worst from someone else's subjective mind with an even more selfish agenda. The intellect alone, with the wrong content, will beat you into submission, falsely telling you negative things that do not serve you. You are not your mind. Your mind is put in your body to serve you, not you to serve it. People have continuously lost this battle with the intellect because of the wrong content injected in them by uncontrollable conditions.

Maybe, just maybe, instead of acquiring the content of your body, acquire the content of your fire?

All content in this universe falls into two categories: fiery content and smoking content. Perhaps try tapping into the fiery one. See what happens.

Allowing your fire's content through, while sifting out the sooty content, is a human being's work.

Knowledge and Information

As the human being is structured—head over heart, heart over leg—so is the process of decision to action structured. The mind informs the heart of the facts and the heart then feels; after the heart feels, the legs implement that feeling.

For example: If your intellect is fed content such as, *The world is a dark place*, that would birth a consequential emotion and corresponding action. Perhaps it will scare you and you will look for a lighter place. But if your intellect is instead fed with this piece of content, *Contained within this seemingly dark world is an infinite light*, you will then be filled with hope and joy, and your consequential action would be to seek with all of your earnestness to find the light in all things.

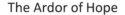

Imagine if all we allowed into our minds was such positive content. What if we fed our minds more positive content and less negative content? We understand that the world is replete with darkness and pain; but just as we control the foods that go into our mouths, we also control the contents that go into our minds.

What if we added one proactive, illuminated, sublime piece of content every day? Just imagine what kind of positive energy this would inspire, and what type of healthy actions this content would produce.

The intellect is like the car's GPS: It directs everything but actually experiences nothing. The intellect leads and determines the emotion. The intellect truly comprehends a matter, but the intellect cannot experience a matter or become it. Intellect is abstract; emotion causes the abstract to become concrete.

Information helps. Content helps. And it does so because of the fire's knowledge you possess, namely:

Knowledge of something is knowing. Knowing is different than information. Information is often bunched together with knowledge. Many people define information and knowledge as the same thing. The difference, however, is that while information is raw data received and downloaded, knowledge is the process of understanding and internalizing that raw information.

For example: That the road is rough and winding is information; this information is your pure content. But knowing how to navigate said road—to adjust your journey accordingly—is knowledge. A meeting of two lips is a kiss, this is information, this is raw content; the electric love that is being conveyed in this meeting of lips, is knowledge.

Your fire's innate ability to develop knowledge allows you to process the light in your content, and this gives you the wisdom to make the correct decisions. Content on its own, without the knowledge of the fire, is potential unrealized.

Back to our automobile: Say you had all the content in the world upon the greatest car body in existence; a supercar that is both faster than anything and also more luxurious; with a driving experience that is smooth as silk and as powerful as ten-thousand horses. Yet, all you do with this supercar is drive it around the same block, over and over again instead of exploring new roads.

This is called content without the knowledge of your fire; this is called energized information without knowing the engine. Content is meant to help your fire burn. Content is not meant to create your purpose, but help it rise.

The Correct Content

This is why education is so essential. You have a fire; education is getting to know it. Healthy education teaches you that the choice is yours.

True, only when one becomes an adult does one truly begin to take control of one's own content. Many children, heartbreakingly, grow up in homes that, at best, do not provide the correct content, and, at worst, provide detrimental, hurtful, dark, and/or abusive content.

If a child grows up in a home with terrible content, it becomes the child's information and the child's norm. The child has faulty content, but this situation is no fault of the child's. The child had bad parenting, or bad education, or bad influences.

To these special souls, we say: Know that it is merely the superimposed content that brings about negative effects; that superimposed content is not your core fire and essential self! Just as negative influences and influencers could feed you negative content, positive influences and positive influencers can feed you positive content. You don't have to change your fiery self; all you have to do is replace your content of blackened coal with content that is on fire, ablaze, alive.

This, in itself, is an empowering message: Your intellect itself—your vehicle itself—is perfect, for the fuel of its engine is fire; all you have to do is change out its content.

As with a car that contains no GPS compass—or, perhaps worse, a malfunctioning system—all that's required is to switch out the bad and replace it with the good, the incorrect with the correct content. So, too, the human being. For whatever reason, some of us have been born or placed into terrible situations, and these provided terrible content. But know that

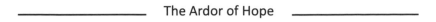

though it might be difficult, you can replace that old, dysfunctional content with new, fresh, state-of-the-art content.

At some point, the conclusion is reached: *This is my own life and I will take ownership of it. I may have been fed poisonous content, but I and my fire do not allow this poisonous content to poison us. My fire and I call it out, flush it out, and burn it out.*

This is the maturation of the awareness of intellect. Life demands it of us, because quite simply this is your soul's purpose, a purpose given—nay, gifted—to you by a greater source. This is the very reason your fire came down into this hearth: to burn and ignite and overcome.

A child knows only the content it has been given. Children are innocent and pure. They are shielded and protected. This is why, if a child is given the wrong content, it is the saddest thing: it becomes the child's entire reality.

But you are not a child. You are an adult. And an adult has the gift of acquiring new content, new perspectives, and new ideas. If you do not feel your fire burning, if you do not feel prosperous, if you do not feel the unforgiving rocks turning into crystal waters, it is high time you changed your content. If you feel hurt and neglected, just change your content. If you feel down and depressed, trade in your secondhand content for true quality.

You are you. Do not allow anyone to dictate otherwise. Your fire burns. And the right content fuels it in a beautiful, awesome, humble way.

Questions Answer

As you read these words, your innate spark flickers and dances and you realize that it's just a question of content and will. You realize there is light where, before, you thought there was but darkness.

The mystics say: A wise question is half an answer. The following questions may help you choose the correct content and find the right answers.

Ask yourself: *Is the content I am about to consume going to make me fly higher or drag me down lower?* If the former, highly regard it; if the latter, surely discard it.

Ask yourself questions that empower your intellect to receive the love and good and not questions that bog you down. Ask not: *Why am I dark?* Ask instead: *How bright can I shine?* Forget the question: *Why am always so down?* And remember the question: *How high can I truly reach?* Question not: *Why do I have so many shortcomings?* But rather question: *Why do I have so much potential, ability, power—for what purpose?*

If your dynamic flame provides your content—and your questions—then you will shine dynamically bright; if however it is your static body, then your answers will reflect statically in kind.

Before consuming the content, ask yourself its source: *Who created the content? Why did they create it? What is the content's purpose?*

Finally: *Is this content going to indulge my body or is it going to feed my soul? Is this content going to stoke my fire or dim its glow? Is this content sourced in and kindred with the essential fire or external things?* Your free will decides which.

Setback to Comeback

You essential Fire guarantees your ability to succeed even in the face of great challenge; and the right content provides the actual tools to do so.

The comebacks, not setbacks, of life define your flame.

As a diamond miner in the depths of the earth, often times we dig and dig, searching and researching for the right content, for the diamonds and jewels, and we are met with setback after setback.

Call them what you will: setbacks, tests, challenges. We have all experienced these roadblocks and detours and recalculations of the road that is life. No matter who you are, the setbacks frustrate, forestall, and confuse you.

But know this: With the right content, the setback is just a prelude to a comeback. The content you inhale becomes the content you exhale to the world. Fellow flame, the correct content feeds your pulsating fire. That ever-growing fire then produces more fiery content by which the world itself is made aglow.

The correct content has fed and nourished the roots of the tree that is your intellect. And right now, right here, is the fruit of that tree. And, get this: The fruits that your tree produces right here, right now, become the content that seeds new trees and new fruits and, ultimately, new fiery content.

The correct content engenders a certain mental toughness. Mental toughness supersedes all setbacks and ensures comebacks from even the darkest places.

The mental toughness of which we speak is not hardness. Hardness, when confronted by an energy force harder than it, is broken beyond comeback. Wood is hardness; wood can be splintered. Rock is hardness; rock can crumble. Glass is hardness; glass can shatter.

Toughness is: *RT—Resiliency Toughness*. No one wears wooden shoes, do they; or glass slippers; or stone clogs. Those materials hurt your feet, restricting movement, causing blisters that won't let you walk—never mind run. Forget about such footwear allowing you to soar.

We wear leather shoes. Leather is tough. Worked leather is even tougher. Rubber is tough; tires on an automobile are rubber, not glass. Toughness wraps around you, hugs you and lets you roll. The right content, like the right tires, creates a toughness, a resiliency that will allow you to first walk, then trot, than gallop, then soar through life while hugging the paths of purpose and roads of meaning.

The correct content—the correct tires and the correct materials—can take any setback and turn it into a comeback. The wrong tires lose air easily and go flat. The right tires provide air and are always well-rounded and complete.

Your fire burns a trail through life. The sublime content you feed it turns a necessary, prosaic commute into a luxurious, poetic journey.

The correct content drives you high and burns you higher.

~~

True content is never truly contented.

CHAPTER FIVE

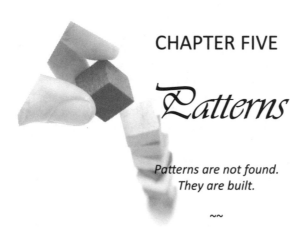

Patterns

Patterns are not found.
They are built.

~~

Hub and Spoke

It is time to build.

We have discovered Fire, articulated Prosperity, dissected Matter and Spirit, and unraveled the Intellect. It is now time to build the system by which our fires shall burn.

Our lives are filled with so many different elements. They can all work in cohorts, like a perfect symbiotic relationship, or they can be completely alien, at odds with each other. When one central theme runs through our lives, all the details mesh and every challenge is but an opportunity for higher growth. But when there is disconnect between parts of our lives—

never mind contradiction—then even the most basic things become chaotic and overwhelming.

The objective is to construct a system, a patterned tapestry that allows every detail to be powered and empowered by the core Fire.

It is imperative to acknowledge and appreciate the hub from which all of the spokes emanate and around which all of the spokes rotate. Without becoming intimate with the Fire, it is difficult to understand how it may pattern outward to illuminate and warm all the elements of life.

With our words and ideas, we have focused on this hub, on the nucleus, the core, the essence, the Fire of who and what we are. Now we shall dedicate some energy to discovering how the hub branches out into all the spokes of our lives.

Ideas are relative. Actions are not. For example: The science of light may be appreciated by a physicist, yet complete gibberish to a child. But the flick of a light switch illuminates the light bulb equally whether a physicist or a child does the flicking. Hence, the real light and tangible warmth is created through Fire's actions, more than its science.

Actions are the spokes that evolve around the hub of an idea. If you think a certain way, you will act a certain way. Surely, there are exceptions to the general rule, but these exceptions do not nullify the general rule.

If you have no core, you have no pattern.

The goal is to create an ultimate attractor pattern. And for that we had to establish the ultimate core, the Fire.

Pattern All

Everything in this universe fits into a pattern. Trees grow in a predictable system, airplanes take off in a certain sequence, the planets and celestial bodies orbit according to specific astronomic rules.

The human being is no different. Breathing, thinking, feeling, eating, sleeping, working, playing—all of our behaviors follow a certain pattern, and all of our living falls into a defined system.

Each unique entity has its own particular pattern because there is a core essence to each object that demands the pattern. Human life demands that the human being eat, sleep, and work. The core of what the airplane is—a flying aircraft that transports objects or subjects from one place to another— demands that it be constructed in a certain way so that it may take off, fly, and land according to certain rules. Otherwise, it would not be an airplane, but a collection of random parts.

The core of every unique thing demands that its structure and pattern follow according to its specifications. The system—the pattern—is the difference between random pieces and a cohesive whole. The system is what allows the core to flourish outward into all parts.

Generally speaking, positive cores result in positive systems, and negative cores result in negative systems. Even one who claims to transcend the system still requires the system of transcendence.

What happens if we apply this principle to the universe? Is there a core essence to all of existence, which demands that all things interact according to a certain pattern? Is there a cosmic system through which all things relate? Is there a universal pattern that connects the tree to the airplane to the celestial bodies to the human being? And if there is such a pattern, what does it look like, and how can we access it?

Relatively Speaking

For the sake of such a stated goal, the concept of relativism—the idea that there are no absolute truths—is rendered obsolete. While we may agree that there are no absolute truths—truths plural—we definitely do assert that there is one absolute Truth—truth singular—a core that runs through everything and unites all things.

Relative thinking is a beneficial tool when comparing one creation to another. It is helpful in understanding their differences. But relative thinking does not set a standard by which all creation should oscillate. If we desire to find the core across all things, relativism must be left by the wayside.

In addition to understanding the patterned relationship between, say, two trees, our goal is to find the relationship between the tree and the airplane—or, more to the point, the relationship between the human being and everything in existence.

A relative approach works when attempting to understand *one* thing; but it does not work to understand *all* things.

Relativism only allows us to understand the world by comparing and differentiating one thing from another. We here seek to understand the commonality that binds all things.

Put another way: Relativism does not create symbiosis, but rather, differences. Our stated goal, to discover the ultimate attractor pattern, also includes creating symbiotic oneness between all things, not fragmented chaos.

Since our goal is to discover the ultimate attractor pattern, where all things click, we must have a tool concurrent with that goal. Relativism is not that tool. To say that a human being is refined relative to a slab of stone, is meaningless. To say that a human being refines a slab of stone, is meaningful.

To understand the whole world, to create an ultimate pattern of all things—an ultimate attractor pattern—we must seek the ultimate tool that would allow us to understand, trust, and be conscious of this objective.

Faith Based

There is an element of faith here. Faith is not religious, dogmatic, or archaic. Faith is simply confidence: the unwavering certainty and complete trust that all things, no matter how disparate they may seem, do in fact connect somehow, someway. Faith is believing that there is a pattern even if at present one may not see it. The first step is to believe that there is a Fire at the core, a unifying essence that unites all things, and to believe that this Fire touches each and every molecule of being.

This type of faith is not devoid of nor removed from intelligence. On the contrary: This faith places supreme faith in human intelligence, and places the onus upon it to ultimately uncover and discover the connecting factor in all things.

Sure, when we look around at today's world we see many contradictions; many realities that seem to be completely disconnected from each other. We see less unity and more dissonance, less clarity and more confusion. Indeed, we see darkness, pain, and hurt. We see shattered hearts and broken promises.

Faith is the confidence that we can change all of this by uncovering the core Fire that is our core souls, and building out the unifying pattern that essentially does exist in everything. Faith is the certainty that when we do this, all of that darkness, pain, and hurt will melt away like an icicle in the sun.

When this nucleus is discovered, we call it Truth.

Truth Full

What is Truth, with a capital 'T'? How do we define it? How do we know it?

Truth is the ingredient that patterns all things. Discover the nucleus of all things, and thereby discover the Truth. Unveil the common denominator running through all of existence, and thereby unveil the Truth. Falsity is the exact opposite; falsity is the ingredient that fragments all things. Here we define Truth as that which unites seeming opposites, and falsity as that which separates and alienates.

What element connects a tree to an airplane, or a fruit to a human being? Is there a pattern, a Truth, that connects all things?

Defined in such a way, Truth must be found in all things. If Truth cannot be found in one thing, that thing cannot connect with anything, so that thing becomes false. If we believe that there is a connection between all things—though we presently may not know the connection—then all things must have that nucleus of Truth that allows it to connect.

Money, then, is not Truth; money simply has Truth embedded deep within it. It also has falsity though. If one taps the core of money, then one taps the

Truth. But if one only sees the surface of money, then one sees something false. If the money unites, the Truth within it prevails; but if money alienates, corrupts, you know the falsity has had its way.

This is why righteous, charitable acts are so profound and meaningful: They demonstrate the connection and commonality between two seemingly opposite entities: a giver and a receiver.

What cannot be Truth? Truth cannot be anything that is compromised or compartmentalized. If something is true for me but is not true for you, then that something is not Truth. By definition, Truth bridges you and me. It cannot divide us.

Truths are realized with time. The only question is: How much time? Some Truths are learned immediately—parents love their children; others take thousands of years—the curvature of the earth, the laws of gravity, and the currents of electricity, among others. The truths are always there. However, it often takes humanity many centuries, even millennia, to uncover it.

Truth is unchanging. Truth is eternal. Truth, then, cannot be something purely physical. Everything that is purely physical fades away over time. Truth, however, solidifies over time. It becomes more pronounced and more nuanced, like a fine wine.

Everything physical dies. The pursuit of Truth is the pursuit of life.

How does Truth work—genuine Truth, not indoctrinated or propagandist truth? And where can Truth be found?

A spark of Truth is buried within every single atom of existence. It is usually buried deep. In fact, the nature of Truth is that it resides in the deepest places. The closer to the surface something is, the further it is from the Truth.

Surface elements divide. Deep cores unite.

Just as the Fire rages within your deepest core, giving off sparks that ignite the various facets of your life, there is a cosmic, universal Bonfire that rages within the center of existence, emitting sparks that embed themselves into every facet, particle, and detail of the universe.

These sparks are the Truth—and they are found everywhere, within every equation of physics and within every chunk of matter. All we have to do is open ourselves up to their possibility, and open the possibility of all things to the core spark pulsing within.

Truth, more than anything else, is contingent on our sublime ability to choose—to choose to look at the surface existence, or at the sparks embedded within.

Pro-Choice

Truth is rather paradoxical. It is everywhere. But for the human being—that is, you and me—to access it, we have to choose to do so. Where is Truth? Wherever you let it in. Going through the motions, even if they were great motions, will never unveil the unifying core beneath. A person may walk down the street, past buildings, cars, birds, trees, sky, and people; he may see them all, appreciate them all, and have no clue that they are all connected, or how they are all connected, or why they are all connected.

How is this possible? Just as one has to learn the alphabet and grammar before one can read or write, one has to learn the world and its core before one can see its holistic pattern.

The first step, then, in building the ultimate pattern, is to make a choice. And *the choice is simple in its depth: Will I look for the spark in every object, or only the coal? Do I want life to evolve around one underlying fire, one underlying Truth, or would I rather a fragmented, disjoined existence?*

Choice is essential for an obvious reason.

Once we do make a choice, we may explore the nuances of Truth. But if we never make a choice, life would be lived merely by default, by proxy. Truth can only be found and appreciated through conscious uncovering of deep sparks, not by default living.

To dictate truth, say in a court of public opinion or by clever argument, is not the path of the innate fire dancing in every person's core. This just gets everyone's blood boiling, circling and interpreting social argument for the sake of personal truth. It is arbitrary. And 'arbitrary' is an antonym of Truth.

Truth may only surface when the surface becomes secondary, allowing the defensive, instinctive, self-preservation tendencies to settle. Truth must be found within, and for that we must choose to look within.

If, however, Truth is always secreted in the deepest recesses of an object or subject, how is it unveiled and accessed?

Wise Tool

If a diamond is secreted deep within the ground, a tool, a shovel, is required to unearth it.

Truth is a diamond embedded within the deepest elements of life. To dig it up, a unique shovel is required. That shovel is called Wisdom.

Wisdom, with its persistent digging, unearths the Truths from the depths of existence. Time tests these proposed truths and either proves their eternity or debunks them as myths. If, over time, a certain element fits into all things, then it is truthful; if it doesn't, then it is not.

The only question is: How much time?

'The world is flat' was a supposed truth that took thousands of years to debunk. The sun god is another example. Electricity always existed. But only recently has its reality been discovered and harnessed. For thousands of years, cultures sacrificed innocent life to please some mythical deity. There have been 'civilizations' that slaughtered the weak, the aged, and those with special needs. They thought it was truthful to throw away those they deemed burdensome to society.

Over time, with wisdom, these are all dispelled as dark falsehood, the opposite of light Truth.

Wisdom in and of itself is not Truth, the same way an art degree is not an artist. Wisdom is the tool to unearth the treasure, but wisdom is not that treasure itself. However, when wisdom is used to unearth the treasure of Truth, the wisdom, too, does become a treasure. In the same way an art degree can help you discover art, wisdom can help you discover Truth.

In all times, from ancient to present, the practitioners of wisdom—Adam, Abraham, Moses, Plato, Socrates, Homer, Shakespeare, Newton, Einstein, et al.—were always people who desired less the surface and more the depth that lies beneath. Not all of these leaders, teachers, philosophers, and writers were perfect, but they all utilized the tools of wisdom and insight to unearth the mysteries of existence, to look for and find the sparks of Truth that reside in the nuclei of all things.

These practitioners of wisdom, quite literally, changed the world.

Did these greats create Truth? No, but their wisdom helped them—and us—discover it.

Of course, throughout history, many perceived truths were eventually shown to be misunderstandings, falsities, or downright dogmatic myths. The world is not flat and the sun god does not exist. Sooner or later these assumed truths simply dissolved like sugar in hot tea—only not as sweet.

For this reason, it is indeed a very cynical individual who suggests that murder could be a tool of Truth. Killing is the exact opposite of Truth. Killing ends; Truth begins. Killing is death; Truth is life. Killing breaks things apart; Truth brings things together.

Wisdom, then, is the fusion of faith and understanding. Faith is the acceptance of a pattern. Understanding is what happens when you uncover it, and wisdom is the tool for doing so.

The axiom we build upon here is that there is an ultimate pattern to all things; the Truth that requires faith. Through wisdom, we can prove or debunk this proposition as we move through life. What connects this thing to that? Why are they now distant from one another? What attracts one molecule to the next? What distances one creation from another? This takes much time and is the process of living.

The result of the process is understanding and knowledge. Three thousand years ago, it would be futile to try to prove or disprove that all things are connected. Today, we pretty much know that they are. Today, though still at the infant stages, through faith and wisdom, we understand and know that the core Fire sparks out in the pattern of all things.

Discovery Channel

Truths are discovered, not built. But patterns are built, not discovered.

Once you discover the Fire, you are empowered to build outward, with action and deed, so that the Fire resonates in all things. It does not happen automatically. Once an architect has a plan for the project, the contractor still must build in accordance with the plans, lest they never come to fruition. The soul Fire is the plan—the blueprint—and action is the contractor that builds it out.

Science, one may say, is the process of discovering the deepest layers of its subject. Through theory, thesis, and experiment, the sciences aim to understand the truths embedded in the worlds they dissect. If a discovery meshes with all else, then it will be considered truthful. If it does not, it will be categorized as false. Any scientist will acknowledge that scientists do not create anything per se; they merely study and discover what has already been created, revealing the results for all the world. Newton did this in his eventual formulation of the laws of motion. It is obvious now, and his work is accepted as proof that gravity exists. We have justifiable proof that we can definitively accept as truth. Although you cannot see or touch gravity, you can feel its effects. Though we cannot smell, touch, see, taste, or hear gravity, we have faith that it is there, and we have confidence in this awesome force. We accept scientific findings even of unseen powers as fact.

How does the human being make decisions and live life? The norm for physical man is to gather physical evidence about the world around, digest that evidence, and live accordingly.

The fundamental weakness of this approach is that the physical is but the tip of the Iceberg. Additionally, every human being has a different set of tools and a different collection of evidence by and from which he or she evaluates. If someone had a wonderful childhood, that person will probably have a wonderful perception of people as the person becomes an adult. But if a child has a horrific childhood, the odds of that child having a horrible perception of the world are much greater.

Is there another way? Perhaps the qualifying factor should be: Will this action unite or fragment; will this path bring things together or make them fall apart?

Similar to a criminal case, where cohesion in witness testimony and forensic knowledge is required to reach a verdict of innocence or guilt, rhetoric alone does not reveal the truth. Yet, the judicial system allows for and is established upon the right for both sides to submit its arguments, and for we the people to hear, analyze, and weigh their merits. For better or worse, to find the truth, rhetoric and polemics are often applied. Rhetoric is not an end in and of itself in a courtroom and neither is it our end here. While not enough, informative eloquence, as opposed to mere performance, could be the impetus for action. Ultimately resulting in evidence and testimony to guide and transform us.

The Fire is the common core that penetrates from abstract to concrete, rhetoric to action, theory to fact, argument to evidence, test to testimony.

As such, why not build your attractor pattern around your Fire? Why not acknowledge the truth of your Fire while allowing everything else to rise into its warm orbit?

Instead of forming the essence of your core by and around the patterns of the world, why not form the patterns of the world by and around the essence of your core?

Text Message

Another key factor, one we have already hinted at, calls for elaboration.

Certain texts have been gifted to the world to help establish and recognize both the innate Fire that burns within each of us, around which our patterns are formed; as well as the cosmic core Fire around which the ultimate universal pattern attracts and forms.

These texts contain Truth and wisdom, and they help us understand how everything in existence is meant to dance with everything else, together in one global ballet.

When one comes across such texts, one knows it. No one has to be told, or force-fed Truth. In fact, if it is forced and unnatural it is probably not Truth.

By the same token, one would do well to keep one's eyes open and heart

aware, lest these texts and their profound messages pass one by.

You see, just like the Truth they carry and convey, these texts are deep and unassuming—they never hold press conferences or hire public relations firms—and if one under-prepared for the light, one may be blinded by, or blind to, its luminance.

With faith, wisdom, and understanding in hand, it is time to begin building.

Pattern Building

More often than not, we build our patterns around elements that are less than ideal. For example, we desire money, so everything we do evolves around that desire. We take jobs that are the highest paying, even if they bring us no satisfaction. And we make familial decisions based on economics, even if they compromise our relationships.

Or, it is possible that we desire something less healthy, like a numbing narcotic, an artificial substance, or a detrimental passion, and all of our actions and movements begin to orbit around that one desired goal.

Imagine if the sciences built systems based on the principle that the world was flat? Or if the mystics built worship around the axiom that the sun was the god and creator of all things? There would never be ultimate unity and truth. Nay, the Truth must precede the pattern, and herein lays the first principle of building the ultimate pattern: Build around a true core, and your pattern will be true; build around a false core, and your pattern will be false.

Picture for a moment that there is a baseline in everything you do, uniting all things throughout your day. Imagine for a second that in all relationships, business dealings, and experiences the empirical Truth leaps forth and a harmonious energy pulses.

This is exactly what happens when you build your personal patterns from your core Fire.

The power and results are so superabundant, transcendent, and exceptional that it may seem overwhelming, even if it is overwhelmingly good. This is why it is advisable to become detail-oriented. Focusing in on the specifics of the pattern helps one implement it.

Then, in the times of serenity and reflection, one may step back and look at the big picture, seeing how all of the pixels combine to form the harmonious beauty of Truth.

Pro Visions

One example of how Truth permeates every detail—and, by-and-by, the big picture—is by presenting facts we can all agree upon.

We need provisions to survive in this material world. We all have to eat. Some of us eat more, some of us eat less; some of us enjoy certain foods, while others enjoy other foods. The differences in provisions are quantitative and qualitative, not existential.

So we agree that we have to have various provisions. Why do we need provisions, food, clothing, and shelter, as well as money to purchase all of these things?

In more primitive times, prior to the age of information, we thought that there was no system to things, no pattern, and no unified reason for why the sun shines or how the crops grow. Why do the rains fall, and why do the dews rise? Why do the trees bear fruit and why do humans eat fruits?

In times past, we worshipped what we could not understand. Pray to the sun to shine, bow to the tree for fruit. We thought that the world controlled us, that we did not control the world; we thought that forces patterned us, not that we pattern the forces.

Today, while we are still ignorant about much of life (most starkly, we have ignorance about ourselves), we know that virtually all things are predictable—from weather, to crops, to stock markets. All we need is the right information, and enough of it. Laws of probability, physics, and biology help us calculate how this predictability works. Understand the pattern and understand the object.

Ironically, the only real unpredictable entity is the human being. Sure, there are behavioral psychologists and forensic anthropologists that will predict

how the human will work—and then the human goes and develops the Internet.

The human being, and the human being alone, has the power to choose by which system he or she desires to live. A human being may very well choose to live like a tree, in a forest, drinking only rainwater, unmoving from his or her place. A human may also choose to live like an animal, hunting, feeding, and building a nest for his or her family, even at the expense of attacking anything outside of the pack.

Or, a human being may choose to live like a human being, defined by seeking the Truth in all things. In anything one does—be it a writer, reader, lawyer, doctor, accountant, salesperson, programmer, athlete, dreamer, professor, retiree, jobless—the most human thing a person could do is find the core Truth in that thing. How does my dreaming unite the world around me and within me? How does my lawyering fuse the parts of existence?

With this information at hand, though it is true that everyone needs provisions, perhaps it is more true—the Truth—that provisions need us. Without sustenance we do not sustain. But without us, sustenance would be meaningless.

In ancient times, we worshipped the unknown forces that we thought patterned life. We called those forces 'god.' Today, we realize that there is but one Truth, a Truth that combines, unites, and creates all things. The sun is there to shine on us, not we on it. Earth rotates for us, not we for it.

We need provisions the same way an artist needs art supplies. We need provisions because within each provision—food, clothing, real estate, money, or anything else—pulses a divine spark that allows us to discover art, fire, and Truth.

Every detail we interact with should not be—and, with Fire, *will* not be—an act of consumption but an act of elevation. When we drink a glass of water with the consciousness of the Fire, we are not merely hydrating ourselves; we are revealing the spark in that glass of water.

This, my dear pattern builders, is how a mere detail creates the ultimate pattern of attraction and beauty.

Demand and Supply

Out of fear, uncertainty, or simple laziness we underestimate our innate ability. We usually limit ourselves. Why is it so compelling for us to have what another has or what another says we cannot have?

Rather than attracting the wrong or undesired outcomes, choose a superabundant life, in which you know for certain, with faith and understanding, the ethereal depth that lives within you. The wonder of this revelation will unleash such power that any outcome is at your fingertips, for you to draw on and draw out. Superabundance is the process of receiving more by believing in more and demanding more. Because the system stems from the soul fire, the energy that can flow into it is infinite. The soul is infinite; you are superabundant.

When you remember that you live in a perfectly choreographed ballet, how your act affects everything, how your step moves another's step, would you ever desire someone else's dance?

If you demand energy, there will be supply; and if you supply energy, there will be demand. If you think the dance is solitary and confined, then it will be; if you think you dance without partners, then you will; if you suppose that your fire burns without influencing the other fires of the world, you supposed incorrectly.

The ultimate attractor pattern, the profound unifying system, tells us that all things connect with all things and all fires orbit around all fires. The challenge solely lies in how to find that connection. Picture the dance with all things, and the dance shall then be.

The system of the universe is nonnegotiable. We cannot choose, for instance, not to eat or breathe. But we can choose to change the world with our eating and breathing.

Sure, we must acquire in order to have; we must accumulate in order to possess. If we are driven to acquire and accumulate in order to fulfill and realize our fire's infinite potential, then the acquiring and accumulation is virtually inevitable, an outcome of a core and a system. But if we desire to acquire or accumulate because we think it will increase our self-worth, then we have another situation.

We do not always know in real-time why certain parts of the system work in certain ways, and we certainly do not always know the connection of one part of the cosmic system to another; but honest wisdom and faith in the unifying core allows us to access the cohesion regardless.

And, ultimately, to understand and know its pattern.

True answers are actually very simple. They are not complex. Successful outcomes are not found by attacking the negatives in our lives, but by exercising the power of the positive. We should not so much *un*wire our beings as *re*wire them, through different actions. The solutions are formed that with freedom of choice direct us to align ourselves with an attractor, the source of all creation, the Truth that is calibrated in its infinite wisdom.

Distract to Attract

When we are miserable it is often because we are not being ourselves. Instead of following the pattern of our own personal fires—and the one general bonfire from which these personal fires all spark—we follow the patterns of the oft-cold world.

Attracting to the ultimate pattern is often contingent upon distracting from patterns that are false and detrimental.

Creating our new—and by new we mean our innate—paradigm is the cure for our old, stale routines.

Powerlessness comes from believing you are at a dead end; powerfulness comes from believing, knowing, and understanding that you are really at the opening of an infinite portal, whose highways reach humbling destinations.

By connecting to this wisdom, you genuinely become friendlier, more successful, and better all around. You are not at the mercy of the world, my friend; but your mercy influences the world. You can change things by accessing the thing that always remains the same—your Fire—and building it out into a pattern for all things, attracting every fringe and fraction into your exquisite tapestry.

By allowing the patterns of the world to create your truths, you are setting yourself up for disappointment; but by allowing your innate Truth, your innate Fire, to create the pattern for all of your life's living, you will be setting yourself up for superabundant success.

A beautiful radiance of energy emits constantly from this source. Our bodies feel it, know it, and breathe it. Simply by being our natural selves, we awaken the miracles present all around us. That is, the miracle present all within us.

The thing we call Fire, flickering Truth, and sparking reality.

~~

Truth creates patterns.
Patterns do not create truth.

CHAPTER SIX

Will

Where there's a way there's a will.
Where there's a will there's everything.

~~

Choicest Parts

You are a city, a mini-universe, a micro-world, a personal planet. You are a city. How do you rule it?

You abound with parts too many to count. From biological build to emotional traits to psychological makeup to spiritual inclinations, your vast metropolis is always pumping. You are a city, and your city never sleeps.

The roads of your city are numerous and the journeys are endless. Your heart may pull you one way, while your mind pulls you another way; your circumstances may compel you in one direction, while your dreams compel you in a completely opposite direction. A desire may lead you down a

beautiful path, while a lust may take you down a path as dangerous as it is seductive, or even addictive.

Choices are made, every moment of every day. Most choices are instinctive and intuitive—a blood cell does its thing naturally, instantaneously; to breathe in and to breathe out is effortless; one need not establish a committee to lift a finger, turn a cheek, or shake a leg. These are subconscious choices and you become aware of them only if something goes wrong.

Then there are calculated choices—decisions weighted by the information you are privy to: Should I invest in this stock? Which brand of undershirt should I purchase: the one that fits better or the one that costs less? Should I order the burger or the deli sandwich, and would I like fries with that?

Both the innate subconscious movements and the deliberated-upon conscious decisions are results of your choice making. If you choose not to lift a finger then you will not lift a finger. A person may even choose not to breathe. Sure, this is not normal and unhealthy, but it is within the realm of a person's ability to choose to be unhealthy and abnormal.

The consequences of choices are fundamental in our choice making. If someone is unhealthy—say, addicted to something or ravaged by an illness—then the choices become so much harder, at times seemingly impossible.

Living never stops. With so many choices at hand, the battle for supremacy over your multifaceted city rages continuously. How do we decide between one choice and another? How to decide which path to walk and which to shun? How do we make healthy, beneficial, righteous choices?

The answer is one word: Will.

Life is war: Living is the battle, earth is the battleground, and Will is the general that marshals you to victory.

For Will Drive

Will is a divine attribute. Will is the voice that says: *I don't have to; I choose to.* Having to do something is human; choosing to do something is divine.

There is nothing in life that one *has* to do. One does not even have to live. One does not choose to be born, but one chooses to remain born. For a healthy human being, living is an easy choice. The alternative to life is not attractive.

An addict does not *have* to shoot up; an alcoholic does not *have* to drink; a leg does not *have* to walk. It's just that for some people, some choices are easier than others. For the addict it is difficult not to feed the addiction; for the leg, whose modus operandi is to walk, it is difficult not to walk. But a difficult choice is still a choice.

Just by looking at it this way we have already been transformed into better people. Everything in life is a choice—some harder, some easier—and every choice you make has direct consequences. Your Will is what compels you to choose to live (or not) a certain way.

Knowing that life is a battle, and is meant to be a battle, is liberating. Too often we believe that life is meant to be experienced on automatic pilot. First of all, there is no such thing; second of all, life is meant to be flown by man, not automated by machine.

The recognition that the battle lines have been drawn, and that the battle never ends, is the first step to victory. Now you can wake up every morning to tackle the challenges and, through your choices, transform them into opportunities.

Choose on This

There is one thing you cannot choose to do and that is: not choosing. Not choosing is also a choice, albeit one that smacks of resignation. Your Will is programmed into you the same way breathing is programmed into you. Just as you cannot choose to stop breathing and remain living, you cannot choose to stop choosing and remain who you are. Like your Fire, your Will is not something you acquire; but something you are.

Your core is Fire. A Fire has to burn. You are a Fire. You have to burn. Your burn is called Will. The only question for the fire is: *What and how will I burn?* And the only question for you is: *What and how will I use my Will? What and how will I choose?*

The ramifications of this are profound. Everything in life is a choice that you have made, making you inimitably unique; meaning that no one else is like you; meaning that you can choose everything and be anything; meaning that anywhere you are right now is by choice; and, more importantly, that anywhere you want to go is by choice as well. No matter your present circumstance, you can always go higher and further.

This also means that you are never really out of control. How did you get here? It is by choices made, most made long before things spun (seemingly) out of control. There was a build-up and lead-in to this chaos. It did not just happen. Those choices made by you, or choices made by others that affect you, have led to this uncontrollable chaos.

More than one would care to admit, every single person, at one point or another, feels as if life is slipping away, out of control, as if one were quickly running out of choices. But if choices were the catalyst in the first place for the present-day hopelessness, then the present-day choices will be the catalyst to once again reclaim the reins of control. By tapping the Will, small step by small step, choice by choice, you will begin to once again rule over your city.

We may at times feel so far away from our own selves that we fool ourselves into thinking we are close. At those times it seems virtually impossible to return to the pure place we knew before.

At that moment, you know that you have to make choices. And it is then that your Will begins to wake up.

Difficult Choices

You are never, ever a victim—always a chooser. Even when someone hurts you, and inevitably someone will, you have the choice of what to do with that hurt. Sure, it gets harder, but that makes you greater. A victim is someone who makes choices without knowing it or without knowing that an alternative choice exists. A victim is someone who believes he is blind when really he can see across the world. Thus we say, you have the Will, and

no matter what anyone tells you, you are the greatest visionary in the world.

Even when one has experienced innocence-shattering darkness, one still has the choice to reclaim that innocence. Only, now it is much more difficult. The question is not: *Do I have a choice?* The question is: *How do I make the difficult choice?*

What then makes a choice difficult? Why are some choices harder than others? An easy choice is one that is aligned with your programmed way of living. Say you give charity every day. Then when someone asks you for a penny, it will be pretty natural to give that someone a penny.

But if you have never given a charitable penny in your life, giving a penny to someone would be one of the hardest things in the world.

Or, say you run seven miles a day. Then, running a mile tomorrow would be as easy and natural as tying your shoes. But if you have never run a hundred feet in your life, then choosing to run a mile will be highly painful, albeit not impossible.

Will, especially a strong Will, is more revealed when one makes difficult choices. Will is needed to run that extra mile.

Will insures that you are never a victim but always a victor.

Will you be a victim or a victor?

Logistics vs. Dynamics

Generally speaking, it is much more difficult to modify one's innate characteristics than it is to adjust one's more external decisions. It is much more difficult to choose to learn to play the piano than to decide where to play it once you have learned. It is much more difficult to choose the right person to marry than to choose when the two of you should get married.

Many of our day-to-day conscious choices are logistical—where, what, when, how, etc. But the deeper decisions—the ifs and whys in your life— are much more subconscious and ingrained. This is why it is essential for a child to be loved, cherished, and educated in a healthy and loving manner.

Then, the child's important life decisions will be so much easier, healthier, and confident.

Some choices, such as time and place, are ephemeral; they matter very little afterward. Others, the ifs and whys, matter a great deal—always. Even more significantly: Why you are where you are and why you are when you are, is mostly not in your control. You did not choose to be born on a specific day, to a specific family, in a specific place. But why you are, and how you will live, is totally up to you.

Most of us lend much energy to logistics decision making, and less to our essential dynamic choices. We think that this is how we will gain control over our lives. We think that by controlling the externalities and logistics of our lives, we can control our internal lives as well. This is a big fat mistake. We gain control by controlling the core choices. We control our logistical lives by choosing to live dynamic lives.

When an adult makes a choice to hurt other human beings, that choice did not begin at the hurt; that choice began when a choice was made a long time ago that allowed room for such a nefarious idea to ever take root.

You do not decide where, when, how, or to whom you are born, but you can—and will—deliberate over how you live and what will be left after you shrug off this mortal coil. The self-evaluation that you can do at any time is that of your Will. The awakening comes when you recognize you are free and responsible. The Will is yours to live. Your Will defines you in your actions. Your thoughts can be chosen. Thoughts that shoot through your mind are learned. They are sometimes acted upon and sometimes not, but your choice of which thoughts to focus on is your Will in action.

World Will

Stop for a moment: If you are the Will of you, then what Will is causing all the universes—including our planet—to operate? We see a linear world, we understand it, and we can calculate it. However, most happenings occur in a nonlinear sphere. We think unexplainable events are random. But, as mentioned in the previous chapter, scientists have now debunked the theory of chaos and now believe that there is a coordinated calculation to every event. Nonlinear thinking is vital to understanding the 'how' and 'why' of

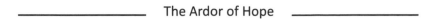
things that happen.

What is the world's Will?

If you, one single human being in the vast scheme of things, are a city that never sleeps, how much more so is the cosmic universe a city that never sleeps? Your city, your world is a microcosm of the world at large, and if the microcosm is ruled by the Will then the macrocosm is ruled by the Will many times over.

If you are constantly making choices, how much more so is the universal body constantly making choices?

If the Will exists in us locally, how much more so does the Will exist in the world globally?

We can catch a glimpse of the Will of the world, the World Will, by inferring from our own Will.

The only reason we do anything is because we choose to. The World Will does not *have* to create anything, but it chooses to create everything. This means that nothing is by chance—especially in our own lives—and everything has consequences. If the World Will chooses to place a blade of grass in a certain position at a certain time, there is a reason for it. If the World Will chooses to create you and chooses to instill within you a Will, there is a purpose behind it.

Having a World Will also means that everything in this created existence traces itself back to the Will. It attracts all things to its purpose. It pushes, pulls, and manipulates all things to its reason. Every known entity in existence is under this great and awesome power.

As you are a sum of your Will and the choices it directs you to make. The world is a sum of the Creator's Will, and the global choices that are made as a direct result.

From time immemorial, humankind has worked diligently to discover what this force may be. Scientists, philosophers, mystics, and cynics have cajoled, experimented, believed, and prayed to understand and connect with this Will. They have dissected and analyzed the world's hows and whys in order to know the Who.

Some believe there is a how and a why but not necessarily a Who; others believe that there is only a Who, but not necessarily a why or how (or, if there were, it is beyond our limited scope).

We submit that, as is the case with us human beings, the how and why of existence is an outcome of the existential Who.

Coming to a Who can only happen by analyzing the how and the why. If you know how the world works, and why the world works, then you can know Who makes it work.

Look at it from this point of view: If you want to know who the person is, look at how the person functions and why the person is. If you want to know Who true existence is, study the Will, by looking at the choices the Will inspires: the how and why of reality.

Ask: *How do heaven and earth connect? Why do heaven and earth connect?* And discover Who connects heaven and earth.

If you know how a computer works, and why a computer works, then you can get pretty close to what the computer is. If you study how the world works, and why the world works, you can get pretty close to Who the world is, the choices it makes, and the Will it begets.

Align Meant

This also means that our own personal Wills are reflections of and fashioned after the World Will. Thus, by making use of our Wills, by our choosing, we are emulating, somewhat, the Creator.

Does this not then compel us to choose wisely and carefully? If this Will creates us, then every choice we make using the Will is earth-shattering, heaven-opening, mind-altering and life-changing.

This awesome power creates and uses itself as a template. You are a mirror image of this awesome power. You, through your actions, become united with this awesome power. The ultimate truth in all things: when you have

the Will to live and thrive, you can do anything and everything that you choose to do with your life.

Just as the choices we make shape our cities, so do the supernal choices form and formulate existence itself. With Will, the Creator chooses to make skies blue and earths brown, to conceal secrets in the most unlikely of places, to reveal profundities when we least expect it, to pulsate life and make it vibrant, to give us our innate Fire and inspire us to burn.

The least we can do is return the favor.

The Creator chooses for us to have a will of our own—the ability to make choices. Why? So that we may align our choices with the Creator's choices, so that our personal Wills may synchronize with the World Will.

Aligning the Wills—or realigning the Wills—is the goal of the Fire.

This is done through our good choices.

Good Choices

The choices really boil down to two: good choices and bad choices. Some synonyms of good and bad are: light and darkness, day and night, love and hate, life and death, heaven and earth, soul and body, spirit and matter, positive and negative, give and take.

If we boil it down far enough, every single choice we make can either be a good choice or a bad choice. Many of these choices are not *what* or *what not* to do, but *how* or *how not* to do it. The question is not: *Should I or should I not drink water when I'm thirsty?* The question is: *How (and why) am I supposed to drink water when I'm thirsty? How am I elevating this water as I drink it? How can this water help me quench the earth's existential thirsts?*

The contrast of good and bad is not only so that we may make choices; the contrast of good and bad is so that we may transform bad into good. Our bodies, our matter, and our selfishness naturally inclines us to feed with greed; a good choice is to realize that by feeding ourselves we may then feed the world—that receiving is only so that we may give.

And here is where Will comes into play. Our Will, our Will for good, allows us to make righteous choices, by-and-by winning the battle and ruling our personal cities with light and goodness.

The more we choose one way, the easier it becomes to continue to choose that way. Imagine that you rolled a wheel barrel through the dirt every day. The first day it would be very difficult; but on day one-hundred-and-one it would be quite easy. Why? Because, with all of your wheel-barrowing and wheel-borrowing, a rut has formed. Getting into a rut is not always a bad thing—not if it's a good rut.

At the same time, staying in a rut is often not such a good thing. One always must grow.

The Sculptor

Good and bad, or positive and negative, or pro-matter and antimatter, are a direct outcome of Will.

Picture a brilliant sculptor laying his magical hands to a block of marble; the end result is a mind-blowing, heart-stopping angel. The sculptor's Will chose to carve, this way and that: an indent here, a polish there, resulting in humbling, innocent beauty.

When the sculpture is complete, there is one perfectly innocent angel and much debris: harsh chips of marble, stone dust—the remnants of the artful carving and sculpting process.

The patron who experiences this work of art has two choices: The patron may choose to focus in on the angel, or on the leftover shards, the mess that the creative process left over. The former is an angelic choice; the latter is a messy choice.

The same is true of life. The Creator, by Will, carved and carved. And the innocent angel of the universe was formed. In the process, much debris came into being, with much chaos, and much noise.

We, the patrons, get to choose: Do we wish to embrace the innocent angel, or indulge on the razor-sharp debris?

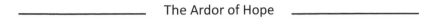

Those who embrace the innocence of life, the angel, have chosen more wisely than those who bloody themselves upon the leftover shards.

Free Will

Truth be told, there is a third choice, the most profound choice of all.

There is the person who embraces the angel, and there is the person who gorges on rubble. Then there is the person who gathers up the skin-ripping shards, works diligently on them, and turns them into a beauty beyond.

This, my fellow Fires, is the highest level of Will: the choice to take the broken parts of life and turn them into angels. This is what we call Free Will. Why is it called Free Will? For one very simple reason: It is freeing.

Unfortunately, evil is very real. No one has to be convinced of this. But our ability to do good—to choose good—is even more real. The debris in the world is everywhere, from World Wars, to terrorism, to hate, to abuse, to bigotry, and to murder. We have the ability and responsibility to sublimate the debris by refining it and turning it into angels.

Will we dedicate our lives to embracing the angel or groveling among the debris? We can win the battle over evil, over the shards, and take control over the cosmic city. With our Will to do good, even (and especially!) in the face of evil—not always the easiest of choices—we align our Will with the Will of Heaven.

With one good choice, we can avenge a thousand bad choices. Choosing to light one fire can warm all the world.

Bad Choices

We here define evil as anything that detracts from the World Will. Murder, the defilement of innocence, is the worst form of evil. That which brings chaos and fragmentation, disenchantment and disenfranchisement (turning angel to marble, angel to rubble), is the complete opposite of the World Will, which is to bring cohesion to all (marble to angel, rubble to angel).

Evil does not have to happen. Evil is a choice. If everyone in the world chose to do no evil, there would be no evil. Our choices do not remain in a vacuum; they affect others. Our positive choices affect others and the world positively. The same is true for our negative choices. We can give birth to life or snuff it out. And when the decision becomes more and more the choice of picking up the shards to turn them into angels, then we can forever eradicate the evil shards of the world, transforming them into works of art.

Someone may be perfect, but someone else may drown that perfection in evilness personified. A child is perfect, unblemished and unsullied; a person may make a choice to hurt that perfection—to take a sledgehammer to the angel. Then, the angel has to spend the rest of its life putting the pieces back together again.

Prescience

But how could evil exist? How could the defilement of the innocent ever happen? Can such things happen? How could anything bad ever happen to someone so pure and good?

The Will—the World Will and the small version living in each and every one of us—precedes both good and evil. There is a part of us—a part right in middle of our innate Fire—that also precedes and predates any evil that may befall us. This means that there is a prescience that gives us the confidence to overcome and transform the rubble into angels.

But the key describing phrase is: *back together again*, meaning that the rubble remembers that it was once together—that there is a point that precedes the break.

Why does evil have such power? This is a philosophical question that would be callous to address in the face of real human experience, nor can addressing it ever justly answer the pain that evil causes. How can a parent hurt a child? How can a supposed human being slaughter millions of other human beings, or even one? The answer is at worst condescending and at best mathematical and thus rendered useless.

A *how* question requires a *how* answer. The answer to a *how* question is a mechanism. The real questions are: *What choices can we Will to forever change the narrative and forever eliminate the evil? How can we go back to the place that precedes good and evil, to forever eradicate the evil?*

To ask *how* evil could happen is the wrong question: Of course evil could happen. Man simply has to make evil choices, the same way a house burns when an arsonist lights it on fire. We do not ask *how* the arsonist burned down the house; instead we dedicate ourselves to insuring that no one becomes an arsonist ever again.

The question that has to be asked is: *What can we do to ensure that the right, healthy, good, holy, and positive choices are always made?*

We all have the good in us. We know this. So our attention should always concentrate on the good and chase away the bad. Evil will never compromise the goodness in this universe. Like a servant to its master, Evil responds to goodness' prescience and goodness' unfathomable power. Inscrutable goodness draws us in and compels us to follow the laws that have been created for us to live in a nonviolent world. By our Will we give a proper response, by obedience to the one true source of all. Why hesitate to heed the calling of this Will? Respond likewise, because you have been created in the same fashion—to simply and promptly obey the goodness that you were created for.

Trust in this wisdom and power of the Creator, Who by the Creator's World Will spoke and all things came into existence, for you to use your Will to see this Source.

This is how we assure good and positive choices, and delete the opposite, forever.

Super Seeds

When we know that the angel precedes the marble, that the Will precedes the choice, and that our Will is rooted in the World Will, everything else becomes commentary: instructions how to turn the present-day battle into the victory of tomorrow.

Once we accept this delicate balance on our own, we can rightly choose the true path of this wonderful production that is playing before us. We trust more. We love more. Our joy supersedes all anxiety that might otherwise threaten to suppress our true selves, in order that we might all partake of this wonderful sphere.

Supersedes—super seeds: when one supersedes the barren elements of life, one fashions super seeds, seeds that, when planted, can sprout the most super and superior trees, bearing the most super fruit.

The divine audience of Will celebrates the choices you make according to the good path you have chosen. Don't get caught in the ego-scripted drama for your own self-congratulatory sake, just because you have a free will to do so. This always leads to self-absorption that serves no greater good.

Our lives—our Will that we were wired with—is not *about* us; rather, it is *for* us. We were not built to command; we were built for obedience, given the prescience of this awesome Will that holds our lives in its hands. We bow, we listen, and we must use our Will to surrender. Then we strengthen our freedom to know, and we strengthen our freedom to exist with a higher meaning. Thus we reject a self-centric, self-absorbed life of meaninglessness that drives us to fill ourselves with seemingly all-important nothingness.

Instead we bow—nay, we lift—to the Will and choose to submit to choice.

Will I Am

The goal is to align the Wills: your Will with the Will of the world, and the Will of the world with everything in it. When you align your Will with the World's Will, you reveal the Will in everything. And when you have revealed the Will in everything, everything is revealed as one.

Making a choice is different than making choices possible. When we make beneficial choices, we tend to think that we invented choice. We haven't invented choice; we are merely utilizing it.

Arrogance is thinking that we create choice; humility is realizing that we use choice.

Have you created life? Have you created your ability to choose? Have you created your Will? If we think yes, we are arrogant and finite. If we know

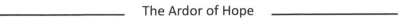
no, we are humble and infinite.

Appearances are not always the same as reality. In fact, they are usually not reality. You appear to be ruling your city autonomously. And, with regard to other people, that is true. You and you alone are the only human being that rules your city.

But with regard to World Will, with regard to the Fire of the world, do you rule your city independently, or do you rule your city as per the guidelines that the World Will has instituted?

It seems as if in the morning the sun rises in the east, and that at noon it hangs high in the center of the sky, and that at evening it sets in the west. But perhaps the sun stands still in the heavens, unmoving all day long and it is we who move: rising, hanging, and setting? Perhaps neither the sun nor we humans stand still, rather it is both of us who are moving? Perhaps all of existence is constantly moving in a cosmic ballet, to a supernal beat, a cosmic cause—a World Will?

In this world of false faces and faux façades it appears that we are the masters of our domain, just because we make choices. But then, what happens when a circumstance hits us? What happens when everything we have ever believed in shatters to the ground? What happens when the angel falls from its pedestal and is replaced by a diatribe of debris?

In the battle for your city, there may seem to be a schism between your will to choose and the Cosmic Will to create: On the one hand you want what you want; but on the other hand the Global Will may want something more sublime and infinite. Our lives must receive the keen awareness that our independence is dependent on this Will of the Creator, and is not dependent upon anything that is created.

Existence itself is Will, and Will itself is existence. By willingly connecting to this, we can truly exist.

True Will cannot be dependent on something. If you make a choice to please your boss, then your boss has the power to influence your choices and, to a certain extent, it is your boss making (or at least altering) your choices.

The only way to make purely independent decisions is to connect to something purely independent. Freedom and liberation is remembering and recognizing that your right to choose—your Will—is rooted in the independence of the Creator's Will.

If Fire is the engine of your city, and Intellect is its pilot, then Will is its torque.

Will it, and it will be.

~~

Willpower is tautological:
Will is power.

CHAPTER SEVEN

Focus

Three parts concentration, two parts vision, one part restraint.
Stir together. Enjoy Focus responsibly.

~~

Focusing In

All ends are possible. The possibilities are endless.

Your innate Fire can illuminate anything, anytime, anywhere; you can achieve whatever you like, whenever you like to, however you like it.

With endless possibilities come endless challenges. If you can do anything, anything at all, what's stopping you from doing nothing, nothing at all? How do you turn abstract possibility into concrete tangibility?

Your Fire is your *why*. When you connect to your *why* you can achieve any *what*.

The only question is: *How? How* do you get from the purpose that is your *why*, to *what* you want?

The answer is one word: Focus.

Focus will show you how to achieve *what* you want, inspired by *why* you are.

By Focal

How does a finger move? What does a finger move toward? How does a finger know to move?

How does a mind think? What does a mind think about? How does a mind know to think?

How does a heart feel? Whom does a heart feel for? How does a heart know when and what to feel?

Focus. Focus is the process of channeling the vast pool of indiscriminate potential into a specific action. Focus is the bridge between the ability to accomplish everything and actually implementing something.

Energy is abundant and could run anywhere. Focus is the process that differentiates one action from another, defining what is primary and what is secondary.

Focus results in here, now, and done; while the lack thereof results in there, later, and processing.

The more you have, the more you have to focus. The parts are piling up, even as the elements are breaking down. Fire, Prosperity, Matter and Spirit, Intellect, Patterns, and Will—how do you stay on top of the game? How do you organize, prioritize, and synchronize? How do you choose what to do when?

Life is packed full with so many elements. How do you know which to embrace, and when?

The answer is on word: Focus. Focus is allocating energy to a specifically designated task.

Take Two

There are two types of focus: There is the instinctive, innate Focus, which comes naturally and takes no conscious effort; and there is the deliberate, decisive Focus, intentionally focusing on one specific task, not another.

In a healthy human being, breathing requires no conscious Focus; the Focus and delineation of energy happens automatically. On the other hand, innovative and unfamiliar tasks, like tightrope walking, chess playing, watch making, or spaceship building, require much conscious Focus.

One need not focus to think; thinking happens naturally. One need very much to focus on *what* to think and *when* to think it.

The first type of Focus, which happens automatically, is no less a miracle than the second type of Focus, which requires manual Focus.

Because the first type of Focus—let's call it Auto-Focus—is automatic, we need not spill much ink on its nature, nor labor, belabor, or elaborate on its implementation.

We shall use our sense and quill to focus on the second type of Focus, the Focus that requires, well, Focus: the Focus that allows an infinite being to hone in on a specific, very finite objective.

As a means for analogy, that magical tool of photography, the camera, could benefit us greatly .

Candid Camera

Focus is naturally associated with cameras. When one snaps a picture, certain elements in the picture are in focus, while other elements remain out of focus.

Cameras come in two general types: digital cameras and manual cameras.

Digital cameras focus automatically on the parts deemed central and important to the frame, like a subject's face. Manual cameras require manual focus: calculated twists of the wrist to bring the desired subject—or object—into focus and blur everything else out.

Digital focus has its advantages. For the majority of things, automated digital focus is preferential, capturing life naturally and without too much concerted effort.

Manual focus has its advantages. For artistic, specialized portraits, manual focus provides a heightened level of nuance and sophistication, creating texture, exactitude, and precision.

In life, too, there are times of automatic focus, akin to the digital camera, and times that call for manual, deliberate focus.

When everything is going right (and may it always), our healthy organic selves—our biological elements, mind, heart, respiratory, and other health systems—are digital cameras that focus and click naturally, effortlessly, albeit unassuming and underappreciated.

Our manual cameras are the difficult decisions we face, the tough choices we have to make: What should we focus our apparatus on? What should we think with our minds? What should we feel with our hearts? Where should we walk with our legs? What should we allow into our mouths? What should we allow out of our mouths?

This is manual Focus. And this is the work of the artist.

Our sublime selves, our Fires, burn perpetually—naturally with or without our effort. This is the digital camera. It is essential but it is not why we are born. After all, it existed before we were born and will exist after we cease being born.

We are born to point our manual cameras at the world, focusing our innate Fire manually and consciously upon the fuel of the world, lighting up the night, warming up the winter.

This is manual Focus. And this is the work of you.

Focus is getting from where you are to where you want to be, by concentrating on and honing in to the specific steps necessary to get there.

The further you are from your goals, the more out of Focus they are. Manual focus and labor is required to attain the desired clarity, to punctuate every nuance clearly and definitively. It is difficult to focus on a face among many faces. But that face is the face you were born to focus on.

The clearer the steps, the clearer the destination; the clearer the destination, the greater the odds of success.

We are ambitious. We desire to achieve Focus across the board, to learn how to focus in any situation, even and especially the nuanced ones.

At War

Focus is a nice concept. But how do you actually Focus? Focus is all about implementation, so how do you implement Focus?

It all has to do with necessity. When you *want* to focus, it is difficult to focus. When you *have* to focus, you will focus.

In times of peace, Focus is optional. In times of war, it is essential.

When you are on vacation, in addition to not having to focus, you probably prefer not to.

When, however, you are in middle of a war zone, or in middle of a boardroom (the urban war zone), Focus would be your preference. One could even argue that you would be doomed without it.

Alternatives do not allow you to focus. When optional, Focus is improbable.

Variety is a blessing—and a magnificent challenge. Variety begets ambiguity. Today, because anything is possible, everything is optional. When you receive an email, because you can *always* read it, you often *never* read it.

This is why specialization is so valued today. Any specialty begins with Focus. When we set our minds to something, to anything, we will accomplish it.

But if we set our minds to everything, we will, in all likelihood, not accomplish it.

But how do you achieve this sense of urgency when nothing is urgent? How do you press yourself when nothing is pressing?

How do you create a groove in a flat surface? How do you create texture when everything is smooth? How do you achieve drive when you feel that you are comfortably at your destination?

War. Effort. A war effort. A concentrated battle. Concentration, like juice from concentrate, implies distilling it all down into one focused, concentrated, and potent product. This is what we need.

The answer is: War.

At Peace

Contrary to your gut reaction, war is not negative. War simply means battle, tension, an adversarial challenge in your way and the struggle—and wherewithal—to overcome it.

Create the dilemma and you will create the innovation. War is the dilemma. Focus will create the innovation.

To focus, you must create warlike situations. What you *want* to achieve has to be something you *have* to achieve. One way of doing this is by making enemies: make failure your enemy, make mediocrity your enemy, make depression your enemy, make second-best your enemy, and make indifference your enemy.

Never make people your enemy.

When surrounded by the enemy, when you know for certain that the vultures of failure, mediocrity, or depression circle overhead, distraction is not an option. When walking on a tightrope, distraction will result in a blunt meeting between your soft body and the hard earth below. When at war, distraction will turn you into a prone target, into easy prey.

The active, proactive Focus of a soldier is the complete concentration necessary for victory. In the war zone of life, urgency is paramount.

Never lose Focus in battle. Remember the rules of engagement, and win. Remember that your Fire must constantly be reborn, that friendly Fire will help you illuminate, and that your Will and Intellect are geared to success. As you battle, be supremely confident that by accessing your innate Fire and mobilizing your unique gifts you will be victorious.

Lines, battle lines drawn from time immemorial and being redrawn perpetually, define the world. One molecule is not another, up is not down, right is not left, cold is not hot, heaven is not earth, body is not soul, and you are not me. There is a perpetual battle between everything, playing the reality of what is against the potential of what could be; pitting the seed of possibility against the tree of fruition, every particle vying for supremacy and primacy. Everything reacts to everything else. Realizing that even the tiniest movement moves the world, forces you to focus on even the tiniest movement.

When you hone into and focus in on this truth, you realize that this type of battle brings about the ultimate peace.

Focus Power

The power of Focus—let's call it Focus Power—is unique to you, the spitting image of Fire. Other creatures, wonderful all, can only focus on what their natures allow them to focus on. Human beings, and human beings alone, can focus on something completely counter to their innate nature.

With Focus Power, a human being who is innately inclined toward haste may slow down, and one who is naturally inclined toward taking it slow may speed up. With Focus, a natural-born procrastinator becomes a well-trained go-getter, and an off-the-cuff firebrand becomes a controlled brand of fire. Focusing on a specific goal, method, or idea allows a human being to achieve it even if it totally goes against one's nature.

Once you activate your Focus Power, every thread of your fiber calibrates toward the object of your Focus Power. You become locked in, zeroed in, zoned in, geared up, honed into, and centered upon your purpose.

Imagine that you did not have the power to focus, that everything was equally sharp. Everything then would be equally blurry. There would be complete flatness, without definition. You would be unable to prioritize. You would be unable to move anything to the forefront or the background. There would not *be* a forefront or a background.

Focus is the difference between a large fire of chaos and a sharp laser of precision. When focused, every tool you possess (Fire, Prosperity, Matter and Spirit, Intellect, Patterns, and Will) is geared toward one objective, consumed with a single and singular goal; all of it committed to a particular utopia. Without Focus, everything becomes anything and anything undefined is tantamount to nothing.

Once Focus Power is engaged, every position and disposition, and every ability and power in your arsenal begins to mobilize. All the legions of honor are deployed to achieve the goal within the sights of your Focus Power. Your Fire burns toward achieving the Focus. Your Will is marshaled by this Focus. Your massive Intellect is driven by this Focus. The Patterns begin to form around the focal point. Every part and particle of your Prosperity feeds the object of Focus. As do the tango-dancing lovers, Matter and Spirit.

In Focus, every molecule in your sphere is committed to one end. The infinite data you have stored since day one is crunched, streamlining according to this awesome and humbling Power.

A laser of concentrated light, your Focus Power slices through obstacles and cuts the appropriate dimensions precisely.

Focus Power is the difference between failure and success, between excellence and mediocrity, and between you doing your best and you doing better.

Universal Term

Focus Power is truth. We know this by how it resonates across a variety of media and within so many fields. Its many synonyms and its countless euphemisms are familiar to you: scientists call it a "flow state"; athletes, "on a roll," or "in the zone"; fighter pilots will say they are "locked-in"; a sniper is "zeroed in," or "locked and loaded."

When you focus, distilling everything into one piercing pith, the powers you once thought great become average, and the things you once considered impossible become routine. You become better than your best. Time moves slower for you while everything simultaneously becomes timeless. When you focus, you do not see what cannot be, only what can. You are on a different plane, and it's never plain.

By whichever familiar term you know it—in the zone, locked-in—this heightened state is the result of your Focus. Like a sniper, where every heartbeat matters because precision is the difference between life and death, where a nanosecond is the difference between success and failure, when you are locked-in you have the power to give life, to sustain worlds, to create a profound genesis out of the barest materials.

Everyone has experienced this, both the sinner and the saint. The saint simply focuses on making things better.

Out of Focus

Focus is a double-edged sword: it focuses on its object of desire and it blurs out everything else. This is important: we have to reach for our goals while simultaneously pushing everything else away.

In other words: Focus is part focusing *on* something, and part focusing *off* of everything else. Focus may be achieved by saying yes to one thing, or by saying no to other things. Usually both are necessary: you have to both focus on one thing and focus away from everything else.

We often underestimate doing nothing. Sometimes *not* doing the wrong thing is as important as doing the right thing. Sometimes, *not* focusing on superficial externalities is as beneficial as focusing on essential internalities.

Soldiering On

Soldiers are the fighters of war. Soldiers are the implementers of Focus.

A soldier is someone who, every day, follows a higher calling to achieve a righteous end. Or a soldier could be someone who slaughters innocent life.

Focus is the difference between soldiering onto a sublime goal and soldering into a hellish pit.

We are all soldiers in this material world. The only choice is: do we soldier on or do we soldier off? We live in war whether we engage or not. Not engaging is a choice as well. Not engaging is a soldier choosing to be a target. We choose a purpose, and so we choose a side. We trade off our emptiness, our hopelessness, and our restlessness for purpose.

When we acknowledge our roles, we commit to our purpose and, like any good soldier, we sign up for our basic and not-so-basic training, entering into the proverbial-but-not-so-proverbial training camp.

Train Tracks

Basic training, as the term *basic* connotes, is just the beginning, the base and basis of your training. The more refined and specialized you become, the more training necessary. The more focused you become, the more focused becomes your training.

Training is honing yourself, submitting to something beyond yourself, and committing to achieving the world. Take a writer or a sculptor; training removes their excess and sharpens their skill. Training educates and aligns the disparate parts, teaching them how to gear together to achieve one focused goal.

Training never stops. A child trains one way, an adult another; an academic trains one way, an actor another; a train conductor trains one way, an orchestra conductor another.

Training seems to be limiting, restraining; but only with training does freedom reign.

Training enables the freedom of your Will to confidently express itself so as to initiate the outcomes of your desire: tailoring a bespoke Will to be an active soldier marching toward the ultimate purpose of birthing your personal freedom. Every professional knows that training engenders confidence to succeed in a specific project or general field. The process demands much energy and focus, but it also gives as much as it demands.

Focus Freely

It seems like a contradiction in terms: by limiting yourself to a goal, you achieve unlimited freedom. Through goal-specific training, you become a well-rounded human being. By locking yourself in, you actually set yourself free.

To the novice it seems counterintuitive: Why break yourself to be complete: is completeness not the mortal enemy of brokenness? Why commit yourself to be free: is commitment not the mortal enemy of freedom? Control and Focus seem to be antonyms to freedom.

Yet, the pianist that trains for twenty painstaking years is the one who plays most freely; the athlete that breaks himself to exhaustion in the gym is the one who ultimately moves unrestrained, unfettered, and fluidly in crunch time. The most focused artist paints the broadest picture.

Focus is freedom's cause. Freedom is the result of Focus.

The soldier in you knows that victory is won by the best trained, the very strong, the very best, the most focused.

Resistance Insistence Instance

The more focused you are, the more the details matter. The greater you become, the more exact and sophisticated you have to be. A mediocre artist is satisfied with being generally good; a master artist cannot have even one flaw. The more irresistible you become, the more resistance you attract. In war, we call this the enemy. It pushes back on everything you push for; it tries to knock you down, sideways, in all directions, every direction but up. You are going up and it does not want you to. You have one path—ascent— and, like gravity, the enemy will do everything in its power to pull you back down to earth.

You cannot easily see this resistance. Like a well-planned ambush, its cause and objective are often well camouflaged. Nevertheless, you know it well and are familiar with its machinations. You are intimate with how it maliciously lies there in wait, looking for your weak points, your tender points, your breaking points.

Every struggle, hourly, daily, monthly, is your resistance. The stronger you are, the more the world seems to be gunning for you. Here is where the players are separated from the spectators. Here is where high-powered Focus factors in. The great ones get greater as the pressure is turned up; the more they need to focus the more they accomplish.

Because resistance is often unseen, do not focus on it but only on your goal. Too much energy is expended on worrying about the enemy; victors do not worry about the enemy, nor do they underestimate them; they simply have greater esteem for success than they do for failure.

You cannot use pain or pleasure to identify the enemy: the resistance may feel pleasurable even though it is really painful; or it may seem like a pain disguised as a pleasure. The resistance is smart, conniving, and shrewd: it will do whatever it has to do to keep you where you don't want to be. The enemy is older and wiser than you; it knows more tricks. Therefore, forget the enemy and focus solely on your soul's success.

When they engage the enemy, the great operatives know that, by becoming an open receptacle through personal commitment to learning and refinement of self, they can achieve victory, transcending the maniacal tentacles of failure.

Failure is a constant. Blurring failure out and focusing on possibilities should become the constant instead.

You will always confront failure. Always. The resistance presses against you so that your well-laid plans come up against the failure you so desperately wanted to avoid. This resistance is in every activity known to every human in every endeavor. There are no exclusions, no exceptions, and no other rules; it is so and always will be so.

The enemy will dog you for every last breath you take. That is the enemy's nature. It knows no other way. Health, finances, and relationships—they are all going to be tested by the enemy of resistance. The battle is on; you cannot choose to turn it off, only to fight it by turning yourself one level higher and being victorious. The failing appears to you in the form of this resistance. It will test you so that you cannot seem to gather it all together.

When there is resistance, you combat it with insistence.

The mantra being: *You could resist my path but I will insist on remaining steadfast on it. I am confident, focused, and insistent.*

Insistence is the opposite of resistance.

In one instant, resistance could be turned into insistence.

Insistence, born of Focus, is the beginning of victory.

Victory Signs

Once your intentions are put to action, the challenges seem to appear out of nowhere. Regardless of how they manifest—as obstacles, confrontations, adversity—they are fueled and controlled by the underlying, albeit unseen, resistance.

While resistance is something that tries to own you, Focus is something you own. Resistance tries to blur your path, while Focus blazes whichever path your heart desires.

Go forth, then, against the amorphous resistance. Stay focused on your goals and trust in your innate ability, perpetually energized by your Fire. Remember, a fire moves inherently, dancing, increasing, and growing. Resistance, is the exact opposite: its aim is to stop you, to cease movement, to cause you to pause, to doubt, to second-guess. This is an enemy. For a soldier at war, one moment of hesitancy, never mind paralysis, could be the difference between life and death. A soldier that stands still is a soldier that will lie still. Your Fire must always move forward, upward, onward.

On the battlefield of life, self-delusion—what is often dressed up in the frilly euphemisms of imagination, false-hope, and fantasy—is catastrophic. Convincing yourself, because it is more convenient and comfortable, that an enemy is really a friend is akin to mistaking a toxic tumor for a beneficial element of growth. It is much easier to believe that you are living on a field of peace than to acknowledge the battlefield of conflict. But, remember: like that toxic tumor, not everything that grows is invested in your growth.

Focus, the active Focus of a soldier, is the antidote to self-delusion. By imploring you to march ahead to victory, occupying your energy and time with thoughts of triumph and actions of achievement, Focus leaves no room for digression.

Before you conquer an enemy, you must conquer yourself. To rule your surroundings, you first must rule your inner workings. Like bench pressing, the more you press up against the weights that push you down, the stronger you become. It is called a workout for a reason: when done with conviction and commitment, it all works out. When finally released, the tension, the pullback, the setback that wants you to stay back, is revealed as the ultimate comeback.

Back Talk

Forward thinking is predicated upon backtalk—that is, *back* talk: less what you have come *to* and more what you have come *back* from. To focus on moving forward, you must also look *back*ward. It is one thing to come to light; it is quite another to come *back* from darkness.

Achievement is found in your comebacks. Setbacks are ubiquitous, what amounts to perpetual push-back against your dreams. We all have setbacks, everyone, and there is no despair in that—unless setting back becomes a modus operandi, unless you do not endeavor to come back from the setback. A setback is a hinderance when it distracts you; it is a help when it motivates you to get back into the ring to fight another round. You do not choose your enemies, nor the directions from which they attack, nor the weapons they use. Every person may be attacked differently. You do however choose to (or not to) fight back. You choose to (or not to) move forward; but it helps to know that, when looking back, you see that you stand on the shoulders of past generations.

Retreat is only retreat if it does not lead to regrouping. Retreat is only retreat if it does not prepare you for a counterattack. Stout defenses are paramount to protect against an attack. But you must also counterattack. The surest way of defeating the resistance is by bringing the war to it. Resistance is great at fighting against others, but it is weak at defending—because it is weak at defining—itself. Resistance cannot resist an attack against its core— its core beliefs and core values. Resistance does not have core beliefs or core values: its core is resistance, not defined goals. Its core is your failure, not its success. Thus, your success would be its failure. Simply by attacking resistance, you have already won. Something that cannot define itself cannot defend itself. And something whose very purpose is *your* failure, lacks its own definitive quality, rendering itself unjustifiable, unsubstantial, and indefensible.

You are on a battlefield, and on a battlefield one best not beat around the bush. Frankly speaking, then: people have low expectations, if they have expectations at all. One may start with a dream, but one often ends up settling for anything that is not a nightmare. Accepting one's plight and passing it off as reality—*it is what it is*—is plain old subjugation to the setback, an apathy born of passive and dispassionate acceptance, playing victim to circumstance.

It is what it is? Never! It is not what it is. It is whatever you make it. Through Focus, it is whatever you make it. And, you can make it like no one else!

I am what I am? No way! You are not what you are. You are what you can become. Say it, feel it, become it: *Through my focus, I am what I can become.*

The give-ups, the quitters, the what's-it-all-mean and who-cares-anyway crowd, are all card-carrying members of the same country club, one whose subpar bylaws limit its exclusive membership to the sub-pars-for-the-course.

Pick up your Focus, your weapon of mass construction, ensure that it is locked-and-loaded, and begin to charge your enemy. Go on the offensive, attack, pursue, be proactive by employing the element of surprise. Standing back is sitting back is falling back; instead, comeback, move forward, proceed, and succeed.

Measure yourself not against others, but against your nuclear self. Give your best to achieve your best and receive your best. Put your best foot forward, put your head down, and charge forth full steam ahead. There are risks involved—that is why many prefer self-delusion—but you are impervious to them. When you lead, you are unafraid of lead bullets. When you shoot forward, you worry not about getting shot.

The resistance desires to put you in *your* place, which is really *its* place. It wants you to turn back, to go back, to backtrack. But when you are attracted you do not get distracted. Indeed, you find that the resistance is part of the solution to your problem. As opposed to putting you down, the resistance drives you to step up; instead of holding you back, it catapults you upward and forward.

Freedom Fighter

You are a freedom fighter, fighting for liberty, fighting to set your self free. An obstacle, a challenge, is a resisting force that tries to tie you down, imprison you, exile your dreams, and enslave your aspirations. As a freedom fighter, your calling is to use every fiber of your inherent freedom to break the bonds, to spread your wings and soar, like a free bird, to places beyond and rarified.

A portion of the combat is head-to-head, idea battling idea, and a portion is hand-to-hand combat, action battling action, using your fingers and fists to fight for freedom. Therefore, attack every obstacle with both your head and your hands.

This philosophy applies to anything you want to achieve. If you want to be, say, a law school professor, you will have to train in the fine arts of law. There will be physical, social, economical, and mental obstacles. To achieve your stated goal, you will have to combat the obstacles with both your head and hands, with both your mental prowess and physical actions, with whatever it takes.

The battle is to stay focused, to never get distracted from your purpose. Anything worth achieving is not handed out, but has to be grasped. The brightest and the fastest, the strongest and the wisest, are not passively gifted their dreams and aspirations; rather, the overcomer, the fighter, the comeback person conquers them proactively. Do not the sit back and wait, but access that energy-driving will of yours, and get that invincible spirit strengthened at every pushback. If and when you take a step back, it should only be to gain a broader sense of where you are and a panoramic view of the battlefield. See every step back as a lens zooming out, up, and over, to help accomplish your purpose.

Say No to No

To the naysayer thou shall say nay. Say nay, and say nay again and again.

Nose are for scenting. The only no you should know should start with a "K." A no is a fly in your ointment.

A no is really a yes that has yet to realize its fullest potential. A no is a yes that forgets its Fire. Simply remind the no about the Fire and it shall heat up, all the negativity melting away like wax in a furnace, pliant and compliant. In the Fire, the no of defeat becomes the yes of victory.

Know yourself, sure, but never no yourself. Do not surround yourself with yes-men or women, but be yourself a yes-man or woman.

Why Fight?

What differentiates an elite warrior from a trainee, a special-opts veteran from a newly-enlisted foot soldier, a superstar athlete from a rookie, or a recognized artist from an amateur dabbler? Focus. Focus is the holy differentiator.

The successful ones are intimate with their *why*. They know *why* they are doing what they are doing. For them, the *why* is everything.

You cannot fight a war and win it if you do not know *why* you are fighting.

If you are in touch with your Fire—with your burn, your purpose, your reason for being, your *why* in this world of *whats*—you will do everything in your power and implement every weapon in your arsenal to focus on realizing your *why*. Without your *why*, you will never focus on anything completely, for why focus on it when there is no *why,* no rhyme and reason to focus on it?

Why is the real question of a true fighter. *Why* are you doing what you are doing? Answer that question, and everything else clicks into place. Don't answer this question, and nothing will fit. Know *why* your Fire burns, and you shall be driven to focus its heat. Know not *why*, and you might get burned.

Impulse is good only once you have the pulse of purpose. Otherwise, it is a wildfire that scorches the earth instead of warming it. The *why* is the eye of the storm and the I of your Focus. If you give yourself the *why*, you can

defeat any problem and find any solution. The *how* comes after the *why*. The *what* is the result. Get the *why*, focus on the *why*, and fight for the *why*.

When you have figured out the *why*, the Focus is clear. Certainty is the truth of the *why*. When you cannot fight with assuredness, more often than not it is because you have yet to discover the *why* of your living: the why-you-are-wanting-what-you-want *why*. If a soldier fights without a cause, without being intimate with the *why*, how could the soldier commit life and limb? Why focus on anything devoid of a *why*?

But when you know *why* (your Fire), you can get *what* (your Matter, your Prosperity) by discovering *how* (your Intellect, Patterns, and Will creator).

You have to fight for something. You need a cause. Imagine that a camera had nothing to focus on: the result is a blur. Do you want your life to be crisp and sharp, or vague and blurry?

As a soldier—and we are all soldiers—you must fight for a cause bigger than your own self. When you get the *why* you get Focus, and when you get the Focus you activate the soldier in you—to march on to overcome, to get the *how*, and to receive the *what*. A soldier knows his duty and, truth be told, you are always a soldier in someone's army. This world was manufactured, not for lone rangers, but for a community of soldiers, for a cohesive army, with a focused chain-of-command and mutual responsibility.

Yes, you are a free individual. But, to achieve transcendant freedom, you have to sign up for something greater than your individuality—not to compromise your individuality but to maximize it. Your choice is in who and what you are fighting for, but you do not have a choice in whether you are a soldier.

To earn victory you must be a soldier. But you do not have to be a robot. You are a person; not a slave, but a free enterprise soldier; not a mercenary to a cause, but a soldier to a cause.

Port Authority

No one wants to answer to an authority figure. Everyone thinks they *are* the authority figure.

In the annals of history, has there ever been a worthwhile achievement that did not require suspension of self for a greater cause? Has a programmer every programmed a program without humbly submitting to code? Has an author every authored a book without lovingly yielding to language? Has an artist ever painted a painting without honorably respecting the pigment? There is authority. The weak try to control it; the strong are in awe of and mesmerized by it.

Authority does not mean an obnoxious boss; authority connotes something higher than your wonderful self, something beyond the ferociously familiar—something more profound than even the profoundest profundity you know.

False authority is corrosive and abusive, and should be shunned. True authority is humbling and empowering, and should be embraced.

People do not like being soldiers because being a soldier implies service, subjugation, humility, suspension of individuality, and giving of self for a higher purpose. Being a soldier presupposes acquiescence to a plan, to a general, to a general plan, to a rank higher than one's own—to authority. A stereotypically unhealthy connotation does not change what authority's true notion is.

The *how* is the authority: *how* to get better, *how* to achieve, *how* to be better than you already are. If your *why* is music, your *what* is musician, and your *how* is your authority: the conductor and sheet music that guides you to symphonic perfection. The *how* is the process of getting what you want.

We all answer to something, whether we like it or not. The only question is whether we are going to answer to something lofty and great, or to something lowly and pathetic. If we have to answer to something, that something might as well be—indeed, it had better be—the most sublime and fiery something we can get our hands on.

If you are a soldier following a general into battle, that general had better be the truest and most righteous authority you could ever know. That general had better be the most excellent general ever.

The *why* of life is the Fire. The *what* is the prosperity and fuel to feed it. *How* you get there is the boss.

The greatest *why*, which begets the greatest *what*, requires the greatest *how*.

That *how* is your Focus.

~~

To blur out the problem
focus on the solution.

CHAPTER EIGHT

Seed & Succeed

A single seed could produce a bountiful harvest.
A single harvest could produce bountiful seeds.

~~

Pre-Seed

It is dirty and brown. It gets under your fingernails, into your hair, and onto your shoes. Insensitive feet stomp all over it. Ignored and neglected, its existence is often derided, forgotten, and underappreciated.

Earth is dirty and brown. Earth gets under your fingernails, into your hair, and onto your shoes. Insensitive feet stomp all over earth. Ignored and neglected, earth's existence is often derided, forgotten, and underappreciated.

Earth is nothing. Earth could be everything.

On its own, earth is nothing. When you plant a seed, earth becomes everything. Brown becomes color; dirt becomes bloom; potential becomes realized.

Earth is both a place and an ingredient. Nothing happens in earth without a seed; at the same time, the seed needs the ingredients for it to become everything.

The seed is the action, producing countless reactions. Every movement we make plants a seed. The only question is: What type of seed—good, bad, or ugly; proactive, reactive, or radioactive? A seed of enlightened truth, or one of diminished falsehood? Do we plant healthy or unhealthy seeds?

By our actions, by the seeds we plant, the earth beneath our toes becomes the heaven above our heads.

Or the hell under our feet.

It all depends on deeds, seeds, and weeds: the deeds we perform, the seeds we plant, and the weeds we uproot.

Pro-Seed

Scratch a tree, and it recovers; scratch a seed, and there is often no tree.

Because seeds are energy concentrate—the result of Focus—every miniscule detail of their makeup is paramount. Seeds are way more sensitive than the results they produce. A mature and stout tree can weather a hundred frosty winters and a thousand blazing summers; a seed cannot weather even one hour of less-than-ideal conditions. A solid evergreen could withstand many blows of the hammer; a seed cannot stand even one poke from a needle.

Seeds produce trees. Trees produce seeds. But a tree cannot produce another tree. The seed is the orb of the tree's potential, its ability to multiply fruitfully and be fruitful in multiple ways. A tree may produce seeds but a tree cannot produce trees.

Size, height, girth, or density is meaningless in this relationship: a seed is tiny, a tree is huge, and yet the seed births the tree.

Thus, the first lesson: one tiny nucleus is the secret to the most luscious garden, one mini-deed could reap a boundless bounty, and one seemingly inconsequential move could change the world.

The lessons do not stop here.

Seed Cycle

Every action you perform triggers equal—sometimes more than equal—reactions. To every inroad you make there is an outcome. For every sequence there is a consequence. Or a hundred.

For every cause there is an effect. This is the law of reciprocity: I give, you take; you give, I take. What goes around comes around; what comes around goes around.

It is called a cycle for a reason. The wheels turn. The only question is: How do you turn them?

See life as a rippling ocean: the more you interact with the ocean the more it ripples. The ripples have a ripple effect, not always perceived but always there. The energies of the ocean of your life oscillate according to the decisions you make: your moves are its movements, your current choices are its current, your stride is its tide, and your acts are its play.

As the gardener to the soil, every decision you make affects the garden. And every seed you plant has eternal ramifications.

This is the give-and-take, the ebb-and-flow, the wax-and-wane, the to and-fro, and the buy-and-sell of life. You cannot receive anything in your life without giving. You will have seeds only if you plant seeds. The more seeds planted, the more trees grown and the more seeds produced.

If you hoard your seeds, hanging them on your walls, stockpiling them in cellars, and placing them in safe-deposit boxes, your seeds will rot and decay into moldy bacteria.

The more you invest in your work, the more your work will return to you. You reap what you sow, and you harvest what you plant. You produce by

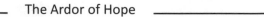

giving what is asked of you—but why wait to be asked. This is obvious: so obvious that it should be stated twice. So we will:

The more you invest in your work, the more your work will return. You reap what you sow, and you harvest what you plant. You produce by giving what is asked of you—but why wait to be asked.

A most fundamental detail is to recognize that everything—every single thing—is a seed. Your thoughts are seeds, your words are seeds, and, certainly, your actions are seeds.

The ripples of your deeds exist on the actionable level. But they exist—and in certain ways, more deeply—on the speech and thought levels as well.

As there are multiple varieties of flora—buds, blooms, flowers, plants, and trees of all kinds—so there are multiple varieties of seeds in your life. These seeds may fall into three general categories: thought seeds, speech seeds, and action seeds.

Thought Process

While an act is concrete and empirical, in many ways a thought is more of an influencer over one's character—and more formative of one's decision-making apparatus—than an action could ever be.

If you spend eighteen hours a day thinking about helping people, the odds of actually helping people are thankfully pretty high. If, on the other hand, you spend eighteen hours a day thinking of hurting people, the odds of actually hurting people are, unfortunately, also pretty high.

Thoughts may not be actions, but thoughts certainly influence and inform our actions. Therefore, every thought is a seed planted. Thoughts are abstract, sure, but they are the first step toward concreteness. Though you can have thought without action, you cannot have action without thought. Your thought is the first step of action.

One may even argue that, by the rules of gravity, the ripples of a thought reach farther than those of an action: because a thought starts at the top, it ripples through all levels of being, influencing everything below it; whereas the ripple of an action, the bottom-line and end-result, requires an anti-gravitational surge to influence the abstractness of the thought above it.

Look at this way: your mind is like the sun. Every thought is like a sunray; it shines down upon the earth that is your body. Every sunray energizes the earth and causes things to grow. Sure, actions on earth can sometimes affect the sun to some degree, but the sun affects the earth below in a more comprehensive and straightforward way.

Your thoughts are like sunrays. Every light beam is another seed planted in the earth of your life.

Sunrays alone, it is true, do not a garden create. For the flourish to happen, one requires the physical planting of seeds and the actionable cultivation of earth and its elements. However, sunrays are the nuclear genesis and solar empowerment of the process.

The same is true with your thoughts: thoughts alone do not a flourishing garden make. Active planting and punctilious earth cultivation are required to actually make the flourish happen. Nevertheless, thoughts are the genesis and empowerment of the process.

Speak Easy

Every thought is a seed, and so is every particle of speech. Every consonant and vowel, every letter and word that flows from your internal factory out into the external universe is a seed planted. Take care to plant the seeds you want to plant. Choose your words wisely. As tailors and carpenters, since the days of yore, are wont to do: Measure twice and cut once. All too often, people measure once and cut twice—and keep on cutting until blood flows freely.

Words are sharp. You must be sharper.

If thought is the beginning of the creative, productive, and procreative process, speech is the expansion of that process. If thought is the depth, speech is the breadth. If thought is the art, speech is the articulation. If thought is a sunray, energizing the garden, speech is the architectural landscape communicating the vision.

Without words, you cannot understand me. With them, the magnificent seeds of collaboration and communication may be planted.

Speech is not action. But, done right, speech may shape and form the most harmonious of all action.

On the flip side, most arguments start with words, not actions. Done wrong, speech can become harsh seeds that could lead to terribly dissonant action.

Start in action and you will end in words; start with words and it will end in action.

Class Action

The most obvious and material seeds are those of your actions. Actions aren't vague; they are absolute. You will not get wet if you *think* about taking a shower and *recite* an ode to the virtues of crystalline waters while standing in the driest desert; however, if you turn on a faucet and step under the water you will get soaking wet, even if you *think* about dry sandy deserts and *recite* dry jokes.

Perhaps thought seeds ripple deepest, and speech seeds ripple widest, but action seeds ripple into waves that actually lap over you and get you wet. *Thinking* or *speaking* about giving charity does not put a sandwich in the hand of the hungry; buying bread, slicing it, slathering it in peanut butter and jelly, and *giving* it to the starved, does. *Thinking* or *speaking* about horticulture does not a garden bloom; *actually* planting seeds and cultivating does.

Action is about getting your hands dirty; action is getting down on your knees with a shovel or spade in hand to turn the soil until your hands blister and your skin leathers in the blistering sun.

Action seeds are the seeds that are the most consequential.

Supplant

We often think more about the fruit than we do of the seed: more attention placed on the product than on the production, the return over the investment, what we take out more than what we put in, the results more than the actions that lead to those results, and the outcome over the input.

This is why we are deathly afraid of frightful death. We worry too much about what will be and not enough about what we are doing to make it be. Your job is to plant seeds, not control results. The more seeds you plant, the less you worry about fruitfully producing. The more you do, the more the results become inevitable. If you have time to worry about reaping it means that you are not spending enough time planting. Those seconds, minutes, hours, days, months, and years you waste on worrying should be spent instead on planting seeds.

Put another way: creating quality is the surest quality control.

If the idea of harvesting crosses your mind, your mind is probably not completely focused on sowing. This will inevitably affect your sowing. Human beings have difficulty with focusing only on seeding, exclusive of fruiting. When you can achieve such a state, you will have achieved ultimate success.

Logically, then, death or failure or mortality should never frighten you: The more you live life, the less you worry about death. The more you plant, the less anxiety. The more you stress action, the less you stress out. Quite obviously: the more you live, the less you die.

The fear of death chains you to your own ego. When it is all about you, you become mortal; when it is all about creating, you become eternal. When you worry about finality, you become less; when you do infinitely, you become more. When you try to hold onto something tightly, you usually crush it; when you let it happen, you will hold it tightly forever. And it will hold you.

Trying to control the uncontrollable creates anxiety, producing more guilt, more shame, more sadness, and, most damagingly, more paralysis. Giving, planting, seeding, tilling, toiling, working, and doing releases you from the constraints of this world. Every single human being, every single Fire, has been gifted a parcel of land, a portion of earth. Magically, the Cosmic Magician and Eternal Gardner has made your existence such that the more you work your earth, the less bound to earth you become. The more you work the earth, the more heavenly you, and the earth, become.

Magic indeed. Or, as the enlightened Fires call it: Reality.

Seedling

If everything you do is predicated upon its presumed advantage, or upon its perceived outcome, everything you do will be predicable and everything you do will be hampered by expectations.

It is difficult to coexist naturally when every move is calculated, when every time you invest you factor in your return. There is a time to calculate, sure, but there is also a time to seed. When everything is calculated, the natural healthiness of human interaction and relationship is marginalized.

Imagine if a seed decided to be selfish, to think only of itself. Imagine if a seed said: *You know what, I don't want to dissolve so that a tree can emerge. I would rather remain tiny, scrawny me than become a flourishing fruitful tree, producing more seeds.* If a seed calculated thusly, that seed would rot and disintegrate. When the seed lets go it grasps the most.

Trying to selfishly control your output impedes you from selflessly committing all your input.

Imagine if, one day, the sun were to shine only on those surfaces that would shine back. The world would cease to exist.

Seeds are meant to be planted. If you have seeds, plant. If you do not have seeds, reach out and grab them. Then plant. And when you do plant, you can never be supplanted.

A Time To...

Time is also a factor. Time is of the essence to sow, but the reaping can never be rushed. Time is of the essence to act, but the reaction may take years. Sowing must be done immediately; but reaping could take a lifetime. And in many cases it does. Sowing is timely; reaping is timeless. Such is the sublime nature of higher consciousness. Myopic visionaries—read:

nearsighted instant-gratifiers—desire quick fixes, fast-food bites, and microwave returns. Those who have reached beyond themselves—read: farsighted long-gamers—know that whatever they put in to the world will reap astronomical benefit—for both themselves and the world—in the right time. It may be today, tomorrow, or in a thousand years. Time is inconsequential. To eternity, time is irrelevant. The eternal people therefore use time; time never uses them. The humble, enlightened, lift time up and never fall victim to it.

If you put a time-stamp, or a reap-by date on your plantings, you will despair. If you do not, you will rejoice.

Many people wake up in the morning with the yank mentality: they crawl out of bed looking to yank on the roots, thinking that yanking might speed up the harvest. Yanking on roots does nothing but uproot your tree and undermine your success.

Look at it this way: the longer it takes for your seed to sprout and your tree to blossom the longer and deeper its roots will be. Be very wary of a tree that matures overnight. Such a tree probably should be yanked out in the morning.

Would you rather have a seed that springs a quick tree with shallow roots, or a seed that nurtures a slow tree with deep roots? Answer carefully.

Live unconditionally, never conditionally. Expectations can work in a healthy way or in an unhealthy way: an expectation becomes unhealthy when it is seen as an entitlement, when you expect to be handed everything; an expectation is healthy when you know for certain that whatever you invest will be returned manifold. The difference between healthy and unhealthy expectations is humility. Expectations based on conditions cause stress. Expectation based on unconditional commitments cause unexpected delights—fruit so abundant you will have to give it away for free, which, of course, produces more fruit, sowing more seeds, ripening into even more fruit.

When your love has conditions it will be a serious condition; when you develop unconditional love for everyone, conditions themselves become conditioned to be unconditional. Anxiety grows from expectations of a flourishing garden without commensurate seeding and tilling. Peace

happens when you spend your long days working the field and knowing—
knowing, not thinking, or even expecting, but *knowing*—that the fruitful
return will surely and assuredly reach far beyond any realistic expectation.

The ground—the earth—has to be watered, and it requires sunshine from
above. Together, the fruit of righteousness grows and ripens.

Seed over Cede

To concede is to yield or surrender to something you do not necessarily
believe in. But what happens if you take the 'concede' and drop the 'con'?
All that is left, then, is the 'cede,' or 'seed.'

A con is a swindle, a scam, a cheat, a fraud. Conceding is acquiescing to
something that is not you, to an imitation (at best) or false representation
(at worst) of the best you. This is the ultimate con. When you remove the
'con' and grab unto the 'seed' you 'succeed.'

Any part of you may be conned. Your mind may be conned into thinking one
thing, conceding to it; but your heart can delete the con. How? The blood
your heart pumps is the ultimate equalizer. The heart and its burn is at the
center—quite literally—of it all.

We plan with our heads. We desire with our hearts. We till with our hands.
This is the head-heart-hand—triple-H—relationship. Your heart is in the
middle, connecting your mind's thought and your hand's action. Your heart
is therefore at the core, the link that connects ideas with actions. You would
do well to plow and plant in a place of your heart's desire.

Naturally,, the heart deserves a chapter all its own. And a chapter all its own
it will get (Chapter Ten). For now, suffice it to say that the heart is where the
matter is. It is called 'the heart of the matter' for a reason.

Thinking, as mentioned, is a seed. But the seed meets earth when a thought
is *acted* upon. And to act upon a thought you need the heart. Logically, to
create a seed you need the mind and its thought; and to plant that seed in
earth you need the heart and its motor.

A mind is not a planter and does not a seed plant. Hearts, however, are defined by automatically sowing the love you have, no matter the thoughts or things you gestate. You may ask: *So, how does this happen?* Consider that your mind always calculates, analyzing and questioning the giving and sowing of seeds into other lives, perpetually wondering what you were created for. This is the mind's job. The heart, which is the essence of goodness, wants to give every bit of your soul to others so as to build them up. This inclination is, in essence, seeds of doing for the other just for the other. In following this inclination, you will receive such a harvest of love, goodness, peace, and prosperity that you cannot contain.

Think about it for a moment: if one tiny seed could produce a mammoth evergreen, imagine the soulfully mammoth evergreen one tiny deed could produce. Put in terms familiar to your innate Fire: one tiny spark can ignite a forest fire, a fire that warms and illuminates the world.

Self-Seed

Self-centered acts are built into every person's DNA. This is your being, and this is even your strength. It could mean that you are full of yourself, or that you are centered. There is nothing wrong with self-awareness. You are created with it. Never apologize for something you are created with; use it instead. Just direct it in the proper fashion. Be extremely self-centered about your life; it is a positive! But it is selfish when it hurts others. That is the wrong application. Be self-centered in knowing that in sowing the good in others, the harvest is one hundredfold for your good. This is proven over and over by testimonies from the ages on down. We get twisted out of shape by thinking it is all about us. Too often, this is what we live. However, the higher thought recognizes in our hearts an unstoppable urge to do for others. We try to fight the urge, thinking: *I must think about me.* Sure, think about "me," how "me" can help others.

There is nothing wrong with thinking about "me." There is something very wrong with *only* thinking about "me."

As a matter of fact, the more someone acknowledges a higher reality, the more one thinks about one's own self and one's own reality. The Fire, knowing that it burns because it is a spark of the Cosmic Fire, often thinks about itself, calculating, estimating how to best burn.

What is my mission in life? How am I to operate each day? On what should I center my focus? You become what you can become only via giving to others. You get what you give. Furthermore, like a seed begets fruit, you get even more than you give. There are thousands and thousands of good sweet seeds to sow. The more seeds you sow, the more the "M" of "me" is flipped, becoming the"W" of "we."

Say *No* to the self-absorbed being, to the myopic being who grasps a grape only to selfishly squeeze out every drop of juice for its own ends, drinking a full-yet-empty glass of lowness and loneliness even as the surround pant in parched in thirst. This is not the life designed for you, nor the one you desire. Your being is crafted to spillover into another's being, to have an overflow of goodness among all, so that as you slake your thirst so do others. You dream and desire and hope for a world where all can partake of the harvest blooming from the seeds you planted, and continue to plant in perpetuity.

To breathe out and exhale into another's lives is liberating; to only breathe in and inhale is asphyxiating. Your calling is to expand outward. This is your life's purpose. Pick a vocation. Pick a journey. Pick a place and breathe life into it by sowing your seed bounty to bloom for the other. Without the other you are alone; with the other you live a life of great fulfillment, sans despair or substitutions. It is up to you to sow into others with the means you have been gifted and the gifts with which you have been overladen. By giving and gifting the means forward, your life burst alive with the energy of genuine purpose, love, and meaning.

Strategy is trumped by seed planting in the financial arena. Why? Because the best laid plans are always uprooted in the face of another, better plan, adapting to the response you receive from the action you give. But a seed blooms regardless.

It seems a lot of worries, or just plain anxiety, pursue us all. When our thoughts are deep in a foundation of giving we become much more creative. More of our thoughts get centered on the provisional aspects of our lives as human beings. This is very obvious. The giving has just plain trust that the unseen universes will supply all needs according to the heart of the sower. When you create a mind-set of sowing financially it is a surrender to the unknown. We do this not for the payback; no one can give themselves to peace and prosperity. This sowing of your financial gain relies on the trust and respect you have that the real purpose of the gift is for the other.

The paradoxical fact is that the harvest is always there. Many people understand this great law, but few exercise it to the point of knowing that a harvest will return. It is the most difficult part of anyone's life. When people make money, keeping it, hoarding is the prevailing instinct. Fear plays this strong. You can never have what you do not keep. Frugality is a good characteristic quality. However, consider the person's concept of living. Seeking the gain of keeping, one becomes a taker. Takers always become the losers to the joy of being. Playing for keeps without shares brings shallowness to the soul.

Expanding yourself to the greater good is all about the giving of the planting of the seed. You can trust the harvest, believe the harvest, expect the harvest, but you can never demand the harvest. If you do, it never runs toward but always away from you. Dominate money, never allow money to dominate you. Money dominates our capitalist society only when the society become obsessed with it. Obsess not over money; rather, obsess over the good you can—and will—do with it.

Synaptic Seeds

Being a Fire at the core influences various parts of you to Fire as well. When your neurons fire, flames leaping from one molecule to the next, another seed is planted. A need seed is planted every time a part of you fires.

The neuroplasticity of the brain is unlimited in its ability to innovate and thirst for learning. Though you may desire run from it, the consuming Fire never runs out. The more varied and diverse your Fire, the more unique its kaleidoscopic hue. Your brain is made up of billions of cells, neurons in perpetual fire. Each neuron has the capacity to transmit copious amounts of energy, data, and information. These neurons are constantly making synaptic connections. Each neuron contains a lot of data and performs countless actions per second. When they make these new connections between themselves, the neurons form into sums greater than their individual parts. How they do this exchanging of electrochemical knowledge with each other is the building of your memory, by keeping these cells connected.

Scientists hypothesize that our brains possess neurotransmitters. Our thoughts are its triggers: the neuron fires a bolt of lightning to the other neurons. This is an obvious simplification, employed to make a point: What you think and how you think creates electric bolts of lightning in your head that fire up the other cells and forms such a signal that you can actually think—which most people call faith into existence the circumstances you choose. It is what you make happen.

Understanding this principle of seedtime and harvest puts you on fire in your mind to receive the harvest, or whatever you want to call it. So stop despairing about your future; you create it every day by what your thoughts are, constantly building your brain into a powerhouse of trust.

Your Fire is always firing, always making connections and planting seeds.

Earth and Hearth

Places are just as important as people. People are in certain places for a reason. Like a vintage wine, terrier and climate have as much an effect on the seed and its fruit as the people cultivating it do.

Every single person has his or her place. If you plant and it does not feel right, perhaps it is time to pick up roots and move to another vineyard. Perhaps it isn't. Perhaps moving is a smokescreen and excuse. Honesty is the only way to know. As is consulting with wise mentors and friends.

It is vitally important to recognize that moving to a new place could be moving closer to your destination, or it could be moving further from your destination.

If a seed does not return the harvest, the culprit could be time, process, or geography. Space and place matter. You cannot receive the harvest if the ground—meaning place—is not returning to you the fruit you plant. Yes, you must move your seed to another place. If one place is barren, another is not. For others, perhaps, a certain acre of earth is ripe for their planting; but for you it just isn't right or ripe. There is nothing wrong with moving, if the moving causes growth and bloom. Moving could be changing jobs, lifestyles, or homes. Moving is good so long as you are moving up.

Geography could also be the culprit. You could be in the wrong place on this planet. Move until you see the harvest sprout. Consider the farmer who plants seed and realizes the fruit will not sprout. One may think that it is a lack of effort or expertise. With more determination and more strategic thinking in this place, perhaps the farmer will succeed. But what happens if the terrier or climate or longitude and altitude is simply wrong?

When you are in the right place, the natural flow makes the harvest seem effortless—less sweat, more fruit, fewer tears, more production.

As earth or geography could hinder your growth, so could people. Negative people could be the weeds or bugs that eat away at your harvest. This is not an excuse to justify unhappiness, rather it is the knowledge that endurance or perseverance is not always the real problem. The unseen universe knows exactly the place for you. Your internal guidance system hones in on this with great clarity. With clarity the world becomes effortless, where it seems that all things are working together for your good. The farmer checks the soil and prepares the soil. The same needs to be true for you in any endeavor.

The wise farmer rises every morning bright and early with the newborn sun, never trying to force his harvest to grow faster by yanking on the roots of his planting but allowing the natural process to run its natural course and take its natural shape. Why? If you pull the seed you plant out of the ground, you disrupt the process and you despair, resulting in an anxiousness that creates less confidence, not more. The harvest will come if you let it come.

Life is as complicated as you wish it to be. Lessons are garnered at the feet of problems. Your soul purpose is to solve problems in the places and plots you are assigned, by maximizing your seed-sowing mind-set. With such mature confidence, you know for certain that the seeds you invest will reap a harvest that shall never divest of its profound and ethereal purpose.

~~

A seed is potential, concentrated.
Those who sow in tears shall reap in joy.

CHAPTER NINE

Solving & Resolving

Look for problems and problems will look for you.
Look for solutions and you will find them.

~~

Problems and Probabilities

The road of life is not smooth. Potholes pockmark the asphalt face along the way. Bumps protrude from the path like obnoxious pimples. The bumps themselves often have bumps. Many challenges and problems arise, and many ditches and craters open before you. To expect life to be smooth is akin to expecting an ocean not to roll, a sea to cease waving.

The goal of life is not to navigate its bumpy road but to turn it into a magnificent highway.

When a problem arises, you arise even higher. When a bump rises, you rise

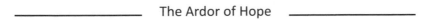

even higher. When a pothole opens up, you open up even more.

As you are born with specific DNA, characteristics, and natures, you are also born with an innate majesty: the ability to solve puzzles. You are a natural problem-solver. You were and are created with a regal dignity, to reign with and rain down hope. It is the human being's gift, wired neurologically into the psyche. You use this wonderful gift to solve any and all problems.

What problem does a fire come to solve? A fire solves the problem of coldness and darkness. Fire is used to transform entities, to cook, to smelt, to fuse. Fire is used to enlighten, warm, and unite. Fire fights wars and wins peace.

Your spiritual Fire solves similar problems: your Fire brings warmth to coldness and light to darkness. Your innate Fire transforms entities, cooking up a storm, turning the raw into the delicious, smelting, fusing, welding disparate parties into one awesome party. You use your core Fire to fight battles, wage wars, and win peace.

You are born with Fire to navigate the bumpy roads of life. But, more importantly—and this may be revolutionary!—you are born with Fire to use it to smooth out the roads and fill in the craters.

You and your Fire, in addition to *traversing* the landscape, are born to *transform* the landscape.

You are born gifted with the spark, and embedded with the sparkle, of the Cosmic Fire—to exist, certainly, but more: you are born with the Fire to burn, to thrive, to innovate.

Survive or Thrive?

There is a world of a difference between surviving and thriving, between existing and living.

Surviving is living *with* problems; thriving is *solving* problems. Existing is about *navigating* deficiencies, *ignoring* weaknesses, and *tolerating* limitations; living is about *transforming* weaknesses to strengths, and *turning* challenges into possibilities.

Your Fire is about living and thriving, not existing and surviving.

This has naked ramifications: You are never a victim but can solve and overcome anything. This too is the epitome of Hope: Despair is born of dead ends; hope is born of trailblazing.

There are two ways to live: Go through life with the parts as they are; or take apart the parts, analyze them, keep the ones you like, dump the ones you do not, and reassemble.

The former is surviving; the latter is thriving.

Being a solver of problems—thriving—means that when you come to the end of the road, you take out your bag of tools, begin extending the road and beating a new path, blazing a new trail and trailing no one.

The opposite—surviving—is, quite literally, a dead end—dead because it is not alive; end because it surely is not a beginning. It is an end that is dead.

Close your eyes and meditate on the profound, heartwarming reality that is born when you see yourself as a problem solver: you will never be intimidated by a problem, for it is, after all, your purpose to solve them; you will never, ever come to a dead end, for every dead end is only a means to a live start. Every challenge is waiting since the beginning of time—yes, the beginning of time—for you—yes, you—to solve it.

When you see yourself as a problem solver you begin to see things differently: any fence is a means to climb higher; any problem is solvable; any barrier is scalable; any mountain is climbable; any obstruction is destructible; any hurdle can be hurdled; any roadblock can be removed; any impediment may be defeated; every obstacle can be obfuscated; any circumstance may be circumvented; any challenge can be met—and then surpassed and transformed. And any schism may, and will, be bridged.

Deal Maker

There are two ways to deal with problems: try to solve them, or rise above them; try to deal with them, or force them to deal with you. Do not play by the problem's rules; make the problems play by your rules. When you play by your rules as informed by your Fire, by a highest reality, the problems will have to adjust to your rules. And when a problem adjusts to your rules, the problem begins to become a solution.

Hope happens when you realize that you are a problem solver. Joy happens when you remember that every bump in the road sends you to a higher place. You happen when you smooth the roads and soothe the pains. Smoothing is soothing.

Timely Solutions

Time does most of the work for you. Wisdom is leveraging time to solve your problems. The mechanism of time is one that, with every tick and every tock, brings you closer to a timeless solution.

Time is on your side. Always.

Problems are portals to higher possibilities. Find a problem, seek the answer, by knowing that hope is something you need not exercise, merely realize. Hope is right with you always. You cannot run from hope. You cannot hide from hope. Hope is there inside you always, wanting to emerge in any problem-solving endeavor you face down.

Without problems there are no solutions. With only problems, solutions become untenable. Problems are a white page before ink hits it; a mountain before it is climbed. When problems are seen for what they are, they give birth to solutions. When problems are seen as problems, they become more powerful. But when seen as the means to a greater achievement, they become weak.

A one-year-old child has a problem: It cannot walk. Over time, with effort, encouragement, and practice, it learns to walk and solves the problem. A few knees are scraped on the way, a few tears are shed, but now the child can walk.

Because the child learned to walk, the child now owns the walking. Because the child learned to walk, as opposed to it being there from day one, the child can now learn how to run, skip, hop, and jump. Because there was a problem, the child solved it and became its master.

If, from the moment it is born, the child knows how to walk, it would take longer for the child to learn how to run. It would be much harder to learn how to run if the child never learned how to walk. It is more difficult to learn algebra if you never learned arithmetic.

Reflect upon the last conversation you had with any one individual. There is a good chance that a problem was discussed between the two of you.

Viewed through this prism, everything in life is a challenge to be met, a problem to be solved.

Finances are a problem to solve. Relationships are a storm of problems to solve. Simply by placing problems in this context, problems already become less burdensome and you become lighter on your feet and lighter in your disposition.

Problem-solve everything: your expectations, your mood swings, your low energy level. Once you realize and acknowledge that you are surrounded by problems, you can surround your problems with solutions. Once you define things as problems to be solved, you have already begun to solve them.

The real problem occurs when you think that problems aren't really problems, or that they have already been solved, or that they are solutions.

The side effect—direct effect, really— of seeing problems for what they are, is a higher purpose and an acceleration of hope. There is a reason to live. More, there is an impetus and desperation to live: a need to solve the world and its puzzles, a need to tackle problems, a need to realize potential, and a need and desire to never submit but always sublimate.

Ignoring a problem is tantamount to acquiescing to it; ignoring a problem is like ignoring a leak in your ceiling. Ignoring it won't make it go away, only make it worse; ignoring it will ensure that the leak destroys your ceiling.

Acknowledging a leak and dealing with it results in a stronger ceiling.

Help Others

Perhaps the purest example of problem-solving may be found in your relationships with the people around you. Helping other people is the surest way to help yourself. Helping others solve their problems helps you solve yours.

The word *solve* and the word *loves* are formed of the same letters. In the lexicon of the logophile, *solve* is an anagram of *loves*, and vice versa.

This implies that when one *loves*, problems begin to *solve* and dis*solve*.

People of greatness are those who solve problems. These are the people we seek out.

Illness is a problem. When someone is unfortunately faced with the problem of illness—and may we all be healthy always—they seek out a problem solver, a doctor to help cure the illness and solve the problem.

The medical doctor's value lies in the problem-solving service that the doctor provides.

We must each find a sphere, a field, which solves problems for the people and world around us. This will solve our personal problems as well. Our value is found in our unique problem-solving skills. Find the problem that you are inimitably good at fixing and dedicate your life to fixing it for others.

Problems you solve for others will create your value to them. People seek out and value those who can get straight to the point of a problem, identify it, analyze it, strategize, and offer up a solution.

This is true with finance: if someone needs money—and who doesn't—this problem is solved by looking for a job, working, and getting paid. With the earnings from the work the problem of finances is now solved.

This is true with love: do not run from love problems. They are your greatest source of joy. Ignore them, and they will become your greatest source of disappointment. The challenge is always there for you to solve. Do not shy away from the oncoming problem train. See and understand it for what it is beneath the surface: a means to an ends, a ladder to great heights, wings to fly.

Realize your dreams, to birth a new beginning. Everyone dreams of a life they want. Why do many live dream-killing lives? Because as soon as you start birthing your dream a tornado of problems is born as well. You become weak and weary because you naturally become negative. To approach each and every problem as the solution to your realizing the dreams you hold is the beginning of freedom from an anxiety-filled life. Therefore, have hope about the problems that arise. They arise from this place of your dream of a better life, not the other way around.

Resolute Leadership

What is the essence of leadership? It is not size, intellect, wealth, charisma, or beauty. It is the ability to solve problems. More than any other quality, people will follow the leader who can solve problems. One may, predictably, think that a leader has it all, that evey leader is the total package, that every quality is at the leader's disposal. But, something to consider: Can that person solve problems? When you want direction or you want confidence, whom do you seek? Of course you seek the one person that's going to give you, or help you find, the answer to your problems. Leadership is about one thing: Leading people from the arid desert they are in to the moist promised land they desire to reach.

By definition, a leader is someone who leads from one point to another. If you are hiking up a dangerously sheer cliff, a leader shows you the way, which steps to take to reach the summit. By definition, a leader is a problem solver. The problem is the mountain; the leader solves it by showing you how to scale it.

The best leaders teach others to lead as well. The best problem-solvers, in addition to solving problems, they teach others to solve problems as well. They will show you how to scale the mountain in such a way that ultimately you will be able to scale the mountain on your own, and lead others to do the same.

The good leader smooths out the path for you. The great leader helps you discover the tools to smooth out the path for yourself. The good leader uses his Fire to blaze an illuminated path for you. The great leader reveals the innate Fire that burns in you, empowering you to blaze an illuminated path on your own, and inspiring you to empower others to do the same.

You are, naturally, a good leader. With hard work, commitment, and dedication, you can become a great leader. And you will.

Nothing is Unsolvable

It is one thing to believe that you can solve problems. It is quite another to believe that you can solve *every* problem.

In this belief is contained the difference between navigating through the bumpy roads of life and turning them into magnificent highways. If the goal is to navigate through bumpy problems, then believing you can solve problems suffices, but if the goal is to turn the bumpy challenges into magnificent solutions, then you must believe that you can solve any and every problem, not just problems in general.

Believing that you can solve any and every problem means that you never have to navigate between problems, because you simply turn those problems into signposts, marks along the fascinating journey of life, constantly propelling you forward.

Many people live an uncertain life, finding it difficult to believe that there is a way to see light in the darkness. Right here, right now, a mission statement of massive proportion, is put forth, for you to declare, loud and clear: *Nothing in my life unsolvable; there is no challenge that I cannot overcome. My health, my finances, my relationships—it doesn't matter, I will solve and resolve to succeed!*

It is incumbent upon you to feel and know, within your internal deep, that you can overcome any complication or difficulty, any comeuppance that may come against you. You might think that some obstacles are simply insurmountable, wondering how a certain break can ever be repaired.

When you feel stuck, at a loss, remember that nothing is harder than your core, nothing is more powerful than your essence, nothing is hotter than your fire. Yes, you can and will solve anything. You were created to do this very thing. Every and all problems are there to solve. It might look like everything is lost: your family, your finance, and your health. But you haven't even dreamed your best dream. And so, you have not lived your best life. It is never, ever. Even when the final buzzer sounds, it's just the beginning of overtime. And overtime is when the game is won. Just believe and declare that any problem you receive, you can overcome. There is just no room to sway from this reality because you are going to help yourself in the first place, and you are going to get the problem solved.

Sense Ability

Most problems are intangible, unseen and percolating beneath the surface. When you walk down the street, you know nothing of the worries, angst, or fears of the people you pass. The same is true with the people that pass you: they know nothing of your worries, angst, or fears. You look happy and satisfied to them and they look carefree to you.

Using the road metaphor: an obvious bump or pothole is easily navigable; a hidden or unseen crack in the road will result in catastrophe. White ice is dangerous but more manageable, because you can see it. Black ice, the same color as the asphalt, is camouflaged and you do not know it is there. How can you prevent skidding on something you cannot see?

You see, the seen problems are dealt with relatively easily because you have no choice; if you don't deal with them you can't live. The unseen problems are the real challenge. They can be pushed under the rug easily; in fact, they already are under the rug.

The service of you and your Fire is to pull the rug from over them: expose the problems, and then solve them.

Learn to trust the sensor inside of you. In your everyday life, the unseen world wants to help you. The unseen wants to prompt you to get the answer. You might feel a still small voice that states the answer. You will hear that stirring inside that says, *Hey, this is what I need to hear.* Sometimes there seems to be an uneasiness you just can't understand. But on some level, you really do know that the prompting you are hearing is the doorway to the answers you need. You just can't ignore this stuff because to solve the problems around you, you know you feel it and you just can't explain it. But you just know the answer.

You don't want to live a life of headaches, heartaches, or bad breaks, but one of joy and love and goodness. You need to rely on this intuition, this small voice, prompting your spirit to say *No* to any problem that comes your way.

This isn't some self-help mumbo-jumbo, or some new-age psychobabble. It might sound a bit mystical. The operative word is: resonate. Some things just resonate; they have the resounding ring of truth. For some of the most important problems you have had, you just had to trust the answer deep inside you that you just couldn't ignore.

Intuition, or instinct, gets you to intuit: to tune in-to-It. This isn't a replacement for hard work, but its result. A highly trained athlete is instinctive precisely because of his or her high level of training. The more you train to solve problems, the more sensitive to them you become, and the more intuitive you become, too. Are you listening to the problems around you? Are you tuned in to what's going on? You may feel anxiously agitated. But you also possess intuition. The universe broadcasts messages that you need, in order to get the solution to a problem you didn't even think was a problem—one of those problems that was hidden under a rug. But you need to do it. You need to heed the impression inside you, or just something stirring inside you, that you need to summon up the courage to face down this problem.

Be in tune and intuit and in touch. The more you work on your intuition, the more you will find that you are in touch and in tune.

At times, something you feel proves to be quite difficult to articulate. This is a result of *trying* to articulate. Sometimes, something just rings true; let it ring without trying to define its ringing.

Alarming Situations

Rrring, rrring, rrring... A smoke alarm goes off when there's smoke. A fire alarm goes off when there's fire. Imagine that there was no alarm: That would be alarming! It would not be conducive to longevity.

Your nervous system informs your brain when something is wrong. It is your personal alarm system, warning when an intruder tries to break in or a dissident attacks your body. It is calamitous if, heaven forefend, an individual's nervous system is compromised. Without feeling pain, one is unaware of the imminent threat on one's being, and an unknown ailment is impossible to treat, cure, or fight.

Your fire alarm goes off when something threatens you. Heed life's alarms and be victorious. A problem is a warning; a problem is life's way of telling you that something has to be fixed.

Nothing is keeping you from your dreams. If something bothers you, do not do it. The problem is there, and fixing it is to have peace. If you don't have peace about it then the answer isn't there. If a decision causes you more indecision there is something wrong. If digesting a piece of content causes indigestion, do not ignore it. When a problem arises, ignoring it will only cause it to continue to rise. If a solution does not include a rise of peace in your being, the solution is flawed. Sometimes you need to listen to what your Fire is saying, to tune into the soluble by hearing the solving and resolving power that lives inside of you. The forces of darkness will try very hard to keep you from fulfilling your destined personal illumination. You were not made to back down and run away; you were made to overcome any problem. And overcoming includes being aware and conscious of which problems to address when. If there is no peace don't go there.

This reel—and real—should be playing in your mind every day. You might feel you are surrounded by all kinds of trouble. But you aren't going to back down. The problem may seem to be bigger than you, but the Fire inside of you is greater than any problem.

There is more *for* you than *against* you. You must keep the right attitude. If you are alive—and many readers of these words are—you have more going for you than against you: You are breathing, thinking, seeing, hearing, reading, acquiring, processing, and developing.

Open your eyes and see how the unseen is much stronger than the problems you can see. And see that you are not weak or intimidated by any problems that arise. You are stronger, with more heart than any problem that threatens to defeat you. You are manufactured to fix the problem, to meet the challenge. The power *inside* of you is much more powerful than any power *outside* of you. You are the most brilliant light that can shine upon any dark problem you have. How do you activate it? By knowing that you are a light that can shine on and in and over and through any darkness.

Not the First

You are not the first person in history to walk down the bumpy road and potholed path. Most likely someone has already gone down this same road and solved the very same problems you are now struggling with. Knowing that someone has been here before and survived diminishes the fear considerably. Knowing that the answer precedes the question, that the solution precedes the problem, that the cure precedes the illness, helps and encourages you. You will always come to problems in life; after all, the road is bumpy. But trusting and knowing that the question already has an answer—and all you have to do is find it—helps erse it from earth's face.

A mistake is not the end, but the beginning. For every mistake you have made, you need to know that this is not the end. Just as you began to make that mistake, you can begin again to solve that mistake. Like building a house, or anything really, if you have done it once you could do it again. This means that if you have made a mistake, you can also make a rectification. If you have created a problem, you can also create a solution.

Never think that it is over. When you walk with authority over your problems you can take out a megaphone and announce to the world that the problem is solved.

Nothing holds power over you. Nothing, save Power itself. And that Power is invested in your success. After all, you are created in its powerful image.

Problems arise, sure, but you are the very definition of rising. You have every bit of the power necessary to defeat anything that comes your way. Stand your ground, look that problem in the eye, and with confidence conquer it. You might feel weak today, but you must still rise up with all the love and passion you have inside of you, knowing that all the forces of the universe can never defeat you.

There are two ways to solve problems: Look for a solution *after* a problem arises; or know that the solution exists even *before* the problem arises.

The former is trying to cure an illness; the latter is the cure preceding the illness itself.

Pain and suffering, and loss and emptiness, are very real. On a personal level, we lose people we love; on an existential level we lose hope; on a professional level we lose our jobs.

But there are two ways to approach loss: as a victor who has lost something dear; or as a loser who has nothing left. The victor, the winner, will ultimately win no matter what, and discover something greater than that which was lost; it is just a matter of time. The loser, the broken, even when he is up is still worried about being down. Approach loss like a winner and you can never lose. Approach winning like a loser and you can never win.

You never were, you are not now, and you never will be a loser trying to discover victory; you are always a victor overcoming a loss. There is a big difference: the former gives life attitude; the latter has a winning attitude toward life.

Higher Fire

An obvious question arises: *If my natural state is victory, where does the drive come from? How do I achieve self-confidence along with drive, and how do I achieve contentment without complacency?*

Don't be discontent about anything. When you are discontent about your life, the problems keep rising to defeat you. Be content with who you are by cleaving to the deepest content possible.

This does not mean that you give up. It just means that you are not fighting everything. You are being strengthened while you are being in the season you are in. Sometimes you work so hard to change a situation that the work itself seems to increase your stress and problems instead of solving them. Know that being content is knowing you are at peace, content in who inherently are, yet never satisfied where you are or how much you have accomplished in this world. Be grateful for what you have and who you are. But never be satisfied or lullabied into believing that you can't be better, go higher.

When you solve one problem, never be content to sit on your laurels and retire. Solving problems is contagious. The more problems you solve the more problems you want to solve. The fewer problems you solve the less you desire to create new paradigms and experiences.

Play vs. Drive

Playing to win is not a drive to win. Playing to win implies that you play the game to win it, but you play the game. A drive to win implies that it isn't enjoyable, it isn't a game; rather, you'd drive anyone into the ground to win, even the ones you love.

This isn't victory; this is tyranny. Driving everything to your win is problem-solving, but it's also problematic.

Play to win and you shall likely win in peace; a drive to win is obsessive, often causing peripheral or collateral damage. It is unbalanced and unhealthy. It alienates the ones you love and the ones who love you.

Do not create more problems on your way to solving a problem. That is like a car driver with a flat tire ramming into many cars on his way to the mechanic. Solving a problem and its process is meant to be peaceful, utilizing the means in addition to the end.

A drive to win gives you a license to use any method, no matter how corrupt. In a drive to win, the ends justify the means. In playing to win, the means create just and justifiable ends.

Soulutions

Why do problems exist? For the same reason that a mathematician has to work out a solution to a complex problem. There are mysteries in this universe, what we may call cosmic problems. The onus is upon humanity, each and every one of us, to dig deep, inquire, challenge, rise, fall, and rise again to discover the truths embedded within, and solve the problems.

The mathematician solves a math problem not because it is an obstacle, but because it is a stepping-stone to greater wisdom.

This is the *why* behind the problem. The *what* depends on the place you are at, the situation you are in, and the person you are blessed to be.

Whatever desires you have, in the context of the greater Will, will allow you to discover a wisdom that seemed unattainable. A problem, then, is something that can reveal a deeper solution. A problem, when probed and pried open, ramifies in improbable development and advancement.

Now, instead of broadcasting that you have a problem, you are happy to announce that you have a solution.

When you resolve to use your soul to solve, you create a soulution—a solution of the Fire that is your soul.

~~

When problems arise, rise higher.

CHAPTER TEN

Heart Burn

A burning heart is different than heartburn:
The latter is an effect, while the former is a cause.

~~

Heart Beat

If you listen very carefully—that is, if you dim the hard noise around you and listen to the soft sound within—you will hear it say that you can change, you can change yourself, and you can change the world.

Now the question is: Do you listen to your heart?

Do you heed the beat that pulses, a rhythm reminding you of how powerful you are? Do you acknowledge when it calls your name?

Certainly actions change things. But so do the emotions of your heart and the thoughts of your mind.

Every action, every word, and every thought is a seed. But an emotion is a seed placed in earth and watered. You can give charity with your hand but not your heart. You can give charity only with your heart but nor your hand. Or you can give charity with your hand as the messenger of your heart.

Your hands and legs are messengers; your heart and mind are the message.

Though we may not see it—and we usually do not—what we think and how we feel affects the matter around us. As modern science has found, specifically quantum mechanics and metaphysics, molecular structures and subatomic particles are influenced by (in addition to one's actions) one's thoughts, emotions, and observations.

As a fire melts iron, glass, and gold, so does your inner Fire shape the world around you. With every flicker, your Fire flecks the world with light.

The Fire within us leads us to action. Even more: as a literal fire's characteristics demonstrate, our inner Fire itself influences and lights and warms the world around us. As such, just by standing still, just by thinking, just by breathing, and just by living, you are warming, lighting, and influencing the world.

Even when a Fire does nothing, it burns and brightens and warms. Just by being, the Fire that is you burns, brightens, and warms the world.

Imagine the level of impact you can have when you actually act.

I Heart You

The mind is cool, calm, and collected. The heart is hot, fiery, and passionate. Mind is objective, scientific, and calculated. Heart is subjective, personal, and instinctive.

The mind-heart relationship is fascinating: the push-and-pull between logic and emotion; the tango of deliberation and instinct; the dialogue—often debate, often heated—between dispassionate matter and passionate spirit. We have all been there, more than once: Heart urges us to grab the opportunity, while Mind cautions us not to be so hasty.

The relationship works both ways: the thoughts of the mind generate the feelings of the heart, and the feelings of the heart influence the thoughts of the mind.

Our biological tendency is to live by following our subjective desires and then use our skilled intellects to justify those desires as healthy for us. The transcendent human innovation is to use our vast intellectual capacity to objectively analyze a situation, forming and fashioning an emotive response accordingly.

In the former, the desire leads to the purpose. In the latter, the purpose leads to the desire.

Our minds are conditioned to rehearse a thought over and over again, which begins to establish a heart condition from mind-thoughts. These mind-thoughts constantly increase heart-strength by purposeful mental programming. Every good and noble thought you repeat will definitely give your heart that jolt that causes a spiritual life of joy, never a body of sadness.

Heart Condition

The best type of heart condition is the conditioned heart. A heart's most well-known product is love. Condition your heart to love. Without this love, one cannot have a warrior spirit that overcomes all of life's setbacks; or, more importantly, a warrior spirit, nurtured by love, will deliver all the desires of the heart. The heart is the resource of the emotional energy that alters universal matter. Change the heart and you will change lives, change your life, and change for and into good all the bad of the world. Rule the heart with the mind and rule the entire body. The heart is empowered by faith that comes from the mind-heart collaboration. It is where all your emotions and feelings will flow from—passion and enthusiasm, and superabundant joy.

A heart is like a horse; love is its rider. Without the horse, there is no ride; without the rider, there is no direction.

Some people think the heart is a mere muscle; it's merely muscle the same way a brain is merely "grey matter." Saying that a heart is but a muscle is like saying that life is an amino acid, a protein. Amino acids are ingredients, not culinary creations. Saying that the heart is "muscle" is like saying ice cream is milk, or that diamond is rock, or that gold is metal: all true, but all missing the point.

The heart is more than a muscle that pumps blood; it is the energy conduit of every cell in your body. The heart can therefore change your perspective of the material world. It is a powerful, incomprehensible energy that can alter the universal laws of attraction.

So, the heart is the energy in the nuclear reactor. The mind builds the reactor; the heart makes it react. The body is the reaction of this nuclei.

How do you get to know your heart, hone it, access it, teach it, learn from it, and make your life more hearty and heartfelt?

Mind over Matter

To understand the heart, we must first familiarize ourselves with the mind-heart dynamic. The mind and heart are in a constant back-and-forth, a dance between the waltz of cool water and the salsa of passionate fire. The collective clarity of the mind is the maestro to the heart's burning symphony.

The mind tempers the heart's fiery lava, while the heart heats the cool steel of the mind. The mind can control the heart's wild stallion, while the heart can break through the mind's ingrained patterns.

The mind, while not ordinary, is orderly, while the heart is the disruptor of order. Order without disruption is a stone-cold hearth; disruption without order is a wildfire that can burn down your house. You need both to warm your life and fuel your living.

This symbiotic give-and-take enables us to overcome bad addictions. We must discern between addiction and habit. Addictions are inherently negative, because they imply that you are enslaved by them. Habits, however, may very well be positive, like habitually being charitable, or kind, or respectful. The give-and-take between mind and heart empowers us to turn bad habits into good ones, and, with hard work, even to overcome enslaving addiction.

The mind is the think tank, living in the realm of ideas; the heart is the battle tank, dealing with the facts on the ground. One is objective fact; the other is subjective reality. The difference between facts and reality is that the former is true in general while the latter is true for you personally. Your mind generates facts; your heart distills them into your reality.

The fact that the sun shines is *generally* true; for someone living in a cellar, however, it is not a *personal* reality. The fact of the sun shining becomes reality only once you enter the sunshine.

The mind knows the fact that the sun shines; but the heart turns that fact into a reality by pulling you out of the cellar and into the sunshine.

Thus, the question is not: *How could a thought and a feeling change the world around me?* Rather, the question is: *How could it not?*

Ins and Outs

When you place increased meaning *behind* your lived experiences, empowering beliefs are formed. When you place increased meaning *before* your lived experiences, you form power.

The internal workings of your being could be influenced by external factors. But less so if you are busy using your internal being to influence the external world. When the current is busy flowing *outward*, less flows *inward*.

It makes complete sense: If an extremity, say a hand or foot, could effect so much general change with a flex or twist, how much more so can your most powerful limbs: your heart and mind!

You mind is your pilot. Your heart is the beat. Your mind cognizes. Your heart recognizes. Your mind registers facts. Your hearts resonates realities.

When we say that an athlete plays with heart, or has heart, it means that he or she will do what it takes: this player will pump and pump until the game is over and won.

Herein lies the concrete import of your mind-heart-action triangle. The pattern of teaching you knit into your mind is the quilt that will rule your heart—mind ruling over heart—and then this becomes "you."

Why is it that success begets success, while failure begets failure? They have both mentally rehearsed over and over what they each feel is normal: their minds have informed, and therefore ruled, their hearts as to what is expected of them—success or failure. The success or trauma is obsessed over, or passionately processed, by the mind until, emotionally, that person's every belief supports the obsession or passion. You are a developer, always developing. Your personality is and becomes your reality. Your personality is made up of how you think, how you act, and how you feel.

The heart is moved by the mind in what we call "realization." Realization, like Focus, has many synonyms: registration, perception, awareness, recognition, grasp, getting it, and savvy.

Comprehension is the positive side of the heart's coin; apprehension, the negative.

Mind is cognition; heart is recognition.

The difference is: mind is an idea *without* you; heart is when that idea *becomes* you.

Hysterical Heart

The mind has the power to influence your heart to the extent that it becomes your reality. This is a very absolute power. Unharnessed unwisely, it can destroy your world. Harnessed wisely, it can change the world.

The key with heart is this: Ensure that you control it and that it does not control you. When something is subjective it is very easily manipulated, easily distorted. And your heart is the epitome of subjectivity.

Use the objectivity of your mind to guide the subjectivity of your heart.

How is the heart so powerful? Its subjectivity is its power. It is geared toward you and only you. You are its everything, its only thing. A heart cannot differentiate between what is good and what is bad for you, but once you decide upon the object of your heart, your heart will obtain it and commit

to obtaining it, regardless. Without mind, therefore, it is only a matter of time before you are enslaved by it. When that happens, your thoughts and feelings clash, creating an existential angst. Only when your mind rules your heart can your thoughts and feelings become one, a oneness that pours through your heart and settles into a seamless peace.

A history professor who has assigned much meaning to his or her studies is so single-minded that the physiological outcome takes on a fixed pattern that becomes the professor's identity. The history professor has never actually *lived* the historical time period of his or her historical study. And yet, the history professor may be more of an expert on the subject than anyone who actually lived through that period of history. The history scholar ends up seeing everything through the prism of history. Or the tech guy ends up seeing everything through the prism of technology, using its jargon and technobabble. Their hearts are fixed to the extent that all choice and experience take on a predictable reality. By controlling the mind-heart destiny, you have ruled your intentions and, thus, your heart.

Wisdom, Understanding, Knowledge

When unleashed, the jackhammering heart-force palpitating along your internal boilerplates, like an earthquake will tremble toward its most desired objective, to finish off its desire. As the earth must leash its internal tremors to prevent natural disaster, so must you leash your internal rumblings. You have a leash tied to your heart that the heart cannot snap: Your mind.

Wisdom, Knowledge, and Understanding are the three pillars of the mind. All else is subsumed under these operational functions. These three pillars control life's responses to distraction, tempering unwanted heart pleasures and unhealthy heart desires. And these pillars also, of course, guide us to enjoy life's healthful pleasures. Depend mightily on these three pillars; they are most important, in order to direct the mind to the right fulfillment of all the passions that your heart desires to grasp. These pillars form and control the patterns of life, both the seen and the unseen layers of existence; they guide the spiritual display within the material facade.

Wisdom is the seed. Understanding is the tree. Knowledge is the fruit. Without seed there is no tree. Without tree there is no fruit. Without fruit there is no purpose. Together, the heart is rooted, sprouted, and driven.

Once all three pillars are exercised and applied, the heart beats accordingly. Then, all that's left, is action—to act upon your mindfulness and heartiness.

This trifecta—a foundation based on a three-point stance— transforms the heart at will. Mind control is mind controlling heart to immerse itself in the sacred acts and kind deeds that better the world.

Repeat, Repeat, Repeat...

By mentally rehearsing, over and over and over again, the transformation of the heart is complete. Your transformed heart will draw to itself the outcomes you have engineered it to pursue. Keeping certain attitudes long enough, by repeating them, will create a concrete belief. When you keep thinking about them, over and over and over again, they become hardwired right into your heart. From the heart pours the very essence of who you have become. The chemical chemistry of your brain—acting, reacting, enacting, repeating—electrifies and conforms your heart to and by its every well-rehearsed thought. Your mind perceptions are formed, achieving a refined state to transform your noble heart.

Why does the basketball player shoot a thousand free throws a day? Why does the baseball player take batting practice for three hours, one hundred days a year? It's called training, ingraining, integrating.

Why does the toddler toddle on two legs, and then two years later he or she can run with reckless abandon? It has become natural with repetition. It is achieving a second nature.

This principle is just as true on the path between your mind and heart: the more you tread it, the smoother it will become; the more you beat the path the more defined and refined the path will be. When you first trailblaze a path from your heart to your mind, the new path is rough: you stumble, get cut, scraped, and scratched; thorns dig into you. The second time, it's a bit better. The millionth time, the path is distinct. The billionth time, you cannot remember that there ever was a time when the path wasn't there. And the trillionth time, the path is a highway.

Can you remember what it was like to be unable to walk or talk? Exactly.

Irrational Heart

Reason has its place. Your mind, your intellect—the mainframe of your being and the most powerful mechanism at your disposal—is completely rational. But so is every smartphone, tablet, and laptop.

You, a human being on fire—a human being who is Fire—also have a heart. As much as your mind is rational, your heart is irrational. Life's most meaningful achievements and most innovative creations do not happen without the irrational. What the masses call irrational, with time and innovation becomes the rational.

In fact, the unseen is the most rational. Proof in point: Can you see an atom with your bare eyes? Of course not. From the eye's perspective, atoms are irrational. But the fact is atoms are rational and anyone who claims that atoms don't exist is rendered irrational.

Irrational simply means deeper reality, unencumbered by the limitations of empirical physical facts. Eternal marriage—happy ever after—is entirely irrational. So is loving a child that is rebellious, or even self-destructive. Thinking you can walk on the moon is ridiculously irrational.

Animals are rational, in a sense that they do what they know. They are predictable; study them long enough and you could predict their every move. Animals are rational: they see the ground, the earth, the here and now; animals are not irrational, in that they do not yearn for the heavens or aspire to fly. The realist says that what you see is all that matters: what you see is what you get. Well, if the innovators of the world believed that what you see is what you get, we'd still be inscribing messages on stone tablets and sending them via carrier pigeon.

Truth is, what you do see is formed by what you don't. The intelligent source has a Will that, if you allow it to penetrate, will pierce your heart, carving into it the secrets of reality too bright for the dull eye of matter to see.

Heart Shackles

Beware of what holds you captive. Whether a noble purpose guides your heart, or an ignoble one, is solely up to you. When a heavenly pump drives your heartbeat, surely then the heartfelt results will be heavenly as well. If however a heart is driven by fleeing superstition and selfish beats, the odds of sublime results decrease dramatically.

Never grow slack in keeping your mind focused on the pattern of higher purposes of creation. Always teach your mind what is pleasing and perfect so your heart is elevated to a level that will guide you to have a warrior spirit to overcome or pursue anything a healthy heart desires.

The most important question you will ever be asked or you will ever ask yourself is: "Who" or "What" does your Fire serve? Your heart serves your Fire, and your Fire serves something, a purpose, a cause, a person, a what, a thing, an idea, a goal... but it serves. Does your heart serve you or do you serve your heart? Or perhaps your heart pumps to a beat beyond? As you mature and your thoughts become centered on what your free will desires, likewise your heart will be influenced by it wholeheartedly. You will become enslaved by your heart's desires because we all are addicted to our feelings. The mind works hard to rule, and at the beginning of our young lives the mind's influence over the heart isn't as strong. That's why what has access to you—parents; mentors; schools; and any phenomenon, thing, or person—matters so much.

Heart Bypass

You must summon every bit of strength you have, to rule your heart so that you can use all your heart to punch back again and again and again. Never quit. Never stop moving. Keep filling your heart with more and more of the stuff that makes it stronger and stronger. You are strengthened by the letters and words typed perpetually on your mind's keyboard. Thus, your heart is strongest when it reads the texts and contexts written and published in real time.

You can be great by choice. You choose what rules your heart—as well as the rules by which your heart plays. There is a tyranny of roles that plays constantly, 24/7, in the mind first, then in the heart. It always goes in that fashion. You can change your heart by what realities you deliberately choose to believe, what data you process, and the information you choose to download. Beliefs are created by repeating the same thing over and over until your subconscious becomes automatic. Then, your heart beats along these ingrained patterns, and patterns new grains into the fabric of matter and existence.

Define and choose your brilliance. You are living a high-stakes mission that is part of—but incomparable to—eternity. You are a specialist with no limitations attached. You want great strengths; you desire to perform tasks better than anyone else. Making assumptions about the future is one of humankind's greatest pitfalls. Your existence stands for something greater than just assuming.

There is, of course, a stockpile of negative information, disinformation, and misinformation that could clog your heart's arteries. The same way your mind must retain positive data and pass it onto your heart, it also must discard the negative data and filter it away from your heart.

With this formula, instead of the world beating down your heart, your heart will beat to a rhythm that could transform the world.

Your heart is calling. It is time to answer.

Heart of Gold

Goodness and kindness are the ultimate equalizers. You can be shallow, dumb, vain, ignorant, foolish, simplistic, complex, whatever. When you are good and kind, every single—and by "every single" we mean every single—problem becomes a solution, every single negative becomes a positive, every downside becomes an upside, every cold darkness becomes a warm light. A heart of gold's currency is goodness and kindness. The price of this gold never goes down, only up, up, upward on and beyond.

Gold is a metal. Metal is hard. Gold is hard but it is also soft. Put gold in fire and it liquefies, pliant to your tools. Place your heart in the proximity of your innate Fire, and your heart becomes the softest thing on earth—so soft it will make everything around it soft as well.

Heartland

When your heart is in the right place, you are in the right place. When your heart is in the wrong place, it is virtually impossible for anything in your life to be in the right place.

Therefore, Focus all your thoughts, energy, and deeds to one goal and your heart will serve for eternity. A heart that beats to a true beat is unbeatable. Eternity is the result. Because you were not created just for eighty-five years and done; you were created for eternity. Be not like the animals of this world, whose eyes are fixed downward to a limited unyielding life, looking only to graze, never to raise. You were created to look up and see the unlimited: the universes that continue on and on.

This is not a one-time event. This is an all-time event. This is a timeless event. For however many years you have left, devote all your time and energy to getting this right, because there is no second chance: it's right here; it's right now. So, what and who does your heart serve? Yes, you carry the heavy gravity of the world on your shoulders. But your shoulders have greater gravitas than gravity. You can and will succeed against the odds.

Before you were born you thought nothing and felt even less. So, what do you have to lose?

Did you honestly believe you came from your mother's womb into this world, and then after a period of time death overtakes you and that is all there is? The human race lives on a thread. Nothing has to be. At any moment, earth could cease to be—no more meaning; born and done.
You really have nothing to lose and everything to gain.

This freedom is heartwarming, freeing your shoulders to bear any load.

Heartthrob

You are a living, breathing organism; your mind and heart are the objective processor and subjective experience. See the world, the universe, and existence, as a living, breathing organism; it, too, has an objective mind processor and subjective heart experience.

If you have a heart, does the world have any less of a heart? No one, not even you, can see your physical heart without piercing layers of epidermis, untangling roped muscle, and navigating tissue. Why then do you propose to see the world's heart without first piercing its outer layers, untangling its hardened habits, and navigating its sinewy interconnectedness? No one can readily see what you are feeling deep inside without endeavoring to discover who you are, so why should you readily see what the world is feeling deep inside without endeavoring to discover what it is?

When you love someone, you yearn to know that someone's heart. When you love the world, you likewise yearn to know the world's heart. If you dare accept it, your mission is to look for the world's heart everywhere, to discover its pulse, and to connect to its beat.

When you *hearten* life, the laughs becomes *hearty*, living becomes *heartwarming*, and life becomes *heartfelt*.

~~

A heartbeat is a rhythm.
Can you dance without rhythm?

CHAPTER ELEVEN

Bridge Building

*Bridges come in two forms: expansion and suspension.
Life requires both expansiveness and suspense.*

~~

Bridge the Gap

Two mountaintops face one another. A raging river rushes between. One mountaintop is covered in prosaic sand and simple stone. The other is covered with the potential of diamonds and gold. You stand on the side of sand and stone. You want to be on the side of diamonds and gold, but you do not know how to get across. How do you narrow the divide and go from where you are to where you want to be?

This is the story of life: You are on one side. Your promise is on the other. An unfathomable gorge separates the two. How do you get from your predictability to your promise, from your routine to your revolution, from your status quo to your desires?

Your dreams are very different than your current reality; your destination is so distant from your point of departure. How do you go from the mountaintop you are on, to the one you want to be on?

You have to build a bridge. A bridge allows you to pass over any obstacles in between, be they raging rivers or enraging insecurities. A bridge enables you to reach farther and higher. A bridge empowers you to span heights, overcome obstacles, pass over low points, and link opposites.

Start on the side you are on, and brick by brick, slowly but surely, reach for the side you want to be on. Bridge building is not a sprint. Bridge building takes time, but its results are timeless and eternal.

When you are stuck in one place, build a bridge.

Bridge Port

Moving forward is scary. Especially if you feel that you are at the precipice of despair. The cliffs are everywhere, presenting limitations and dead ends that impede your progress. You want to proceed and grow in life, but how could you, when a sheer escarpment stands before you?

The cliffs take many shapes: insecurity, anxiety, work, personal life, professional life. They all boil down to thinking that you are stuck on one side. This is the definition of enslavement. Every human being experiences this. It could be a self-imposed mental or emotional cliff that chains you into a prison of asphyxiating proportion. It could be environmental influences. It could be the negative presence of unhealthy people in your life. It could be habits, circumstance, walls and cliffs of menace that confine you.

Most slavery today, most cliffs, are manufactured in the mind and have rooted itself into a very deep place of unrepentant, unforgiving, disbelief.

As an architect designs a building with various means of access and egress, so are you designed with various means of access and egress to reach beyond your perceived limitations. As a computer scientist encodes software with adaptable flexibility, to update in real time and evolve with the ever-changing hardware and technology, so are you encoded by the Cosmic Programmer with perpetually evolving software: engineering that empowers adaptation to any situation and the means to build bridges and traverse any schism.

You are built with something different, a tool and program to get you beyond the tool of your present limiting programming.

We are creatures of habit. Prediction was programmed into you. But so was innovation, newness, genesis, and reaching beyond. Your cliffs are your predictions and limitations. Your Bridges are the abilities to go beyond them.

Both come naturally to you. We often remember that the cliffs come naturally. It is time to recognize that the Bridges come naturally as well.

And by 'naturally,' we mean miraculously.

Came Bridge

Place any physical item under a microscope and you will see that it is comprised of many disparate parts: intricate molecular structures, some that inherently bind, and many that do not. All together, the numerous details make up the whole. What to the naked eye seems to be a seamless object of matter, is revealed to the trained eye as the collective sum of many parts.

The human being alone has trillions upon trillions of parts: copious quantities of cells forming proteins and other substances; inner and outer layers of which it is physically comprised. When you stand back, you see the complete body; the closer you get, the more its definition and detail is exposed.

What connects all the different, sometimes contradictory, parts of existence together? What binds together the various parts that make up one organism? What glue keeps you together personally? What binding agent keeps the world together cosmically?

The answer: bridges, binders, and connectors—factors whose very role and purpose is to fuse the parts. Just as parts were and are created, so are the bridges and binders that connect the parts.

If you break it down into its simplest terms, life is all about bridge building:

discovering the building blocks and clicking them into place, parts merging, molecules binding, links fusing, and bridges uniting what was previously separate, if not disparate.

In addition to building the organisms themselves, these bridges also connect one stage of life to another; seed to tree; tree to fruit; fruit to fruit salad; fruit salad to mouth, digested into energy as fuel for living. Each one of these steps metamorphoses into the next by the means of a bridge, a synapse.

These bridges take us from potential ideas to implemented actuality, from thought to speech, speech to action, and action to reaction. Mind and heart are connected via a bridge, as are fire and firelight, and matter and spirit.

Great expectations become tangible events of greatness only by the means of a bridge. The idea of goodness becomes the substance leading to good deeds only by means of the bridge. You become the best you can become only by means of the bridge.

Anything that develops into anything else – sand to glass, glass to windows or spectacles or wineglasses—only by way of the bridge.

As the grains of sand on the beach, or the glittering stars in the heavens, or the molecules in existence, bridges are in the trillions; infinite, really. Two entities may be bridged in countless ways. Something as humongous as two planets or as tiny as two molecules may be bridged in an infinite number of possible ways.

And how you bridge a schism creates a whole new dimension. Creation and creativity happen when you bridge.

Bridge Stone

By definition, when you are in one place you are not in another. When a student is in grade school, the student is not in high school; and when in high school the student is not in college.

When you are at an entry-level position, you are not the CEO. When you are here, you are not there. When you are now, you are not then. This is a rule of physics.

The question is: How do you get from here to there? No human being is content. If you have one, you want two; if you have a million, you want two million. Standing still is moving backward.

You are here, so it says on the map of your life. Where you are is what you know. It is frightening to leave what you know behind. Where you are is every place you are not. When you are in your living room, you are not in your kitchen. When you are in your kitchen, you are not in your car. When you are outdoors you are not indoors. When you are in Hell you are not in Heaven.

How do you get from the proverbial Hell to the profound Heaven? You have to build a bridge.

After you acknowledge that you are *here* and that you desire to be *there*, the next step to building a bridge is to build a mental bridge.

Mental Bridge

Knowing where you are and where you want to be is the first step of bridging. The second, is building a bridge in your mind.

You begin constructing by deconstructing. Stop thinking in the manner you have been thinking up until now, and open your mind to think differently, innovatively. Thinking in the ways that you thought before, like a cliff, will impede you from moving forward and thinking innovatively. Mental manacles, cerebral chains, sophisticated shackles, brainy barbed wire, wise walls, and polemical prisons enslave you to the comforts of where you currently are. It is an act of subscribing to only one way of thinking and never being open to another. You cannot lay a foundation without first digging up and removing the dirt.

Only once you begin to build a mental bridge—a diagram in the mind of how you want to get to somewhere else—does the next step of actually doing so become reachable. The task is still tough, but it is now reachable, or at least graspable.

Have your mind ask: *Do I really want to be here, on this mountaintop of sand and stone, and not on that mountaintop of diamonds and gold? Do I truly want to be on a mountaintop that feels like the bottom of a canyon of despair? Why do I have to be here, when I want to be there?*

Burning Bridge

Conventionally, burning bridges refers to cutting off from your past, making retreat or return impossible (without rebuilding the burned bridge, in any case). But we are not conventional. For our discussion, burning bridges refers to putting your Fire into bridge building, to making a conflagration of the gaps, and firing-up the bottomless voids: build a bridge by your Fire's burn!

Trees remain rooted in the same spot in the same garden in the same land all their lives. That's great, if you're a tree; but it's the opposite of great if you are a human being. You were not born to remain rooted in the same spot for all of your life. You have to move. You have to aspire to new gardens and new lands. You cannot stand still, you have to walk, run, leap, and fly. You have to bridge; you must be expansive. You must spread your wings. You are born to birth newness, to bridge out to uncharted territories, unbeaten paths, innovative inroads, imaginative beginnings, in acts of creative genesis.

It is scary. It is exciting. It is the cayenne pepper in your dish. It is what makes you. It is your Fire. It is you, forging bridges, illuminating, warming, and flaming your life with the bridges of fire.

Fire's very nature is innovation. The only place that Fire does not burn is where things have already recently burned. But other than that, Fire doesn't stop. Fire is never content. Fire is never nostalgic for yesterday, but rather, it eagerly crosses over to the other side, incessantly, never looking back. Fire fuses, bridges, and welds constantly. Fire burns wild on the crude and raw materials of the untouched and the unprecedented. Sure, Fire could burn on the predictable heart or conventional candle. But Fire could just as easily bridge out and burn on any flammable surface.

First, see the Fire in your mind. Then make the Fire in your life. Visualize Fire burning: a bonfire, a pilot, a blowtorch, a stovetop, or a fireplace. Then visualize it growing, improving, and achieving. Feel it getting hotter, without stop—hotter and hotter. See and feel Fire as it never stops; hear it, as it always crackles and pops, sizzles and snaps, always bridging gaps, searching out new frontiers, conquering new lands, burning new paths, and blazing new trails.

You are Fire. Fire is you.

The unbreakable mental chains of stagnation, of staying put, is caused and created by many factors: bad environment and angst, wrong mental programming and worse heartache, hardwiring and soft laziness, utter fear and otherness, Stockholm syndrome, paralysis, and torment. The surest, if not sole, way of leaving all of this behind is to build a bridge—to irrigate by reaching deep, beyond, beyond the deep.

If you are depressed, build a bridge out to hope. If you are broken, build a bridge out to wholeness. If you are a sea of sadness, construct a bridge to the sure shores of joy.

When you feel like you are nowhere you need a bridge to somewhere.

The bridge to somewhere leads to everywhere and it is the antidote to the effects of being nowhere. The tools to build this bridge are at your disposal; as is the assurance that it will not crumble. As is the belief that, contagiously, one bridge will lead to a million bridges.

Simple: You are here. You see over there. Build a bridge. And another. And another. And another, until every element of existence is bridged and united; every cliff transformed into a foundation, every chasm morphed into a catalyst of new possibilities; every schism the canvas for serendipity and serenity.

Hi Point

As your point of departure—where you are—is important, so is your point of destination—where you want to be.

Without knowing where you are, it would be quite impossible to begin building a bridge. Where would you begin if you don't know where you are? Without knowing where you want to be, it would be quite difficult to ensure that you end up in the right place. How sad would it be to spend all this time and energy and resources on bridge building and bridge crossing, just to end up in the wrong place?

Building a bridge from one prison to another is not the objective. Building a bridge from exile to freedom is.

Cross Examine

After the bridge is built, it is time to cross it. Building a bridge is tough; crossing it may be tougher. Many bridges have been built, left uncrossed and neglected. Sadder than a wide divide and bottomless gorge is a bridge left untraveled, overgrown with thorns and brambles.

Sadly, for every chasm, there are as many neglected bridges; for every void, there are more forgotten viaducts; for every finger of continuous disconnection, there is a hand of discontinued connection.

Building bridges without crossing them is like building a house and not living in it, buying a car and not driving it, having a brain and not thinking, or having a heart and not feeling.

Many great people have lost the battle of the mind because they forgot to cross the bridge. They did not know—or perhaps were afraid of—how surprisingly easy it is. For them it became more and more complex. They were great men of reason, very wise, great thinkers, but they lost the battle because they could not or would not cross the bridge from where they were to the place where they wanted to be. They built the war machine but never used it to achieve peace.

At a certain point you have to stop thinking and start crossing. Yes, you must build intelligently; but you also must stop building intelligently and simply start traversing tangibly.

It's not just the smart ones that lose this battle: it is the person who is homeless as much as those with homes, the brokenhearted as well as the wholehearted, the downtrodden along with the upright, the financially successful as much as the destitute—doubt is egalitarian, indiscriminate, politically correct, praying upon all races, classes, and creeds. Trapped on the one side, tormented by angst and fear: *To cross or not to cross? To not to cross or cross?*

There are so many mind bridges to cross over, but still we fear and doubt and become discouraged. O, how tortuous this life can be: how meaningless and how hopeless, with constant upheaval and relationships fraught with brokenness.

In a capitalist society, people are often measured by the money they have earned, the power they have achieved, or the societal place they are in. We look at the financial bridges we or others have crossed and we jump to conclusions; we judge people, ourselves included, by the power bridges we or others have spanned.

Sure, one may have crossed one bridge, but there are so many more to cross. To measure ourselves, or any person, solely by a single bridge, be it financial, beautiful, or otherwise, is to hone in on one tiny spec at the expense of the vast galaxy. The fighter, the warrior, the fearless overcomer, the persistent forward-marcher remembers that bridge-crossing never stops, that once you reach the other side and conclude one journey it is but the beginning of the next.

It goes without saying, which therefore must be said loudest: judging others is not the domain of man or woman. Rather, perhaps the measuring stick by which each person should judge him- or herself is: *How many bridges have I crossed? How many bridges have I burned with my Fire?*

Sometimes the challenge isn't visualizing or building the bridge. Sometimes the challenge is crossing it. And sometimes the challenge is to never stop building and crossing bridges.

Forget every difficulty. Forget every challenge. Forget every hardship. Forget it all for a moment. Think instead of one thing: crossing a bridge.

One of the underlying problems with problems is their all-inclusiveness: a problem isn't a problem so much as a blanket that covers your entire being in the coldly cynical embrace of the problem. A problems embrace can crush or suffocate. When you are down and depressed, it isn't only your brain or your eyes that are down and depressed; it is your entire being.

Therefore, forget about it all for a moment. Concentrate on one thing—and one thing only. That thing is crossing the bridge. Put one foot in front of the other. Begin crossing. And never stop.

Walk the Bridge

The reasons for not crossing a bridge that is right in front of you, one that you can clearly see and will surely get you across to the other side, where the diamonds and gold are, are multiple and multifaceted, even diametrical:

Fear of heights: you could be petrified of reaching higher, to a place beyond your own usual self, to a place unknown and unpredicable.

Fear of falling: sometimes you don't try to cross, to reach for your potential, because you are afraid of failing and falling.

Fear of the unknown: though you may see the other side, the Promised Land, actually *living* in the Promised Land is a whole other story. Sometimes we prefer the known prison over the unknown freedom, the familiar darkness over the unfamiliar light.

Maybe you hesitate to cross the bridge because you are afraid you cannot afford the toll? Realize that the toll you pay by *not* crossing is way higher; it will take a toll on your life.

The only way to overcome these obstacles, whatever the obstacle may be, is with action. It may take mental prowess and calculated intellect to build the bridge; but it takes straightforward, uncalculated action to cross the bridge. It is as simple as it sounds.

Bridge Funding

To cross a bridge you must trust it completely. No one will drive a car unto a bridge whose pillars and engineering are suspect. Neither should anyone drive a life unto a bridge whose foundations are unreliable. When crossing over from where you are to where you want to be, ask yourself: *Can this bridge's engineering, planning, materials, foundations, and construction hold and support me as I journey to the Promised Land of my vision?* A bridge must be strong enough to withstand your crossing. A bridge must be confident, and you confident in it, to uphold the heavy baggage we often carry around—the kind of baggage with which life burdens the traveler.

Reading, watching, and listening to the news, you digest tragedy after tragedy. Every negative piece of data scares you into playing life safe. *Why cross a bridge when so much could go wrong? People have failed in their aspirations, why then should I venture out unto a limb that holds no guarantees? People and the ships of their dreams have crashed against the rocks; they could not meet their goals, why should I be any different?*

For the same reason that you trust your mind to think and your heart to feel, you should trust your legs to cross the bridge. If you did not trust the quality of your mind, you might be afraid to think. If you did not trust the quality of your heart, you might be afraid to feel. When you trust in the quality of the bridges you have built, you will cross without a second thought, embracing the pieces of daily joy and true satisfaction accumulated along the way of your crossings-over.

You must not then accept the "you" that can live with and tolerate a "less-than" level of worthiness. That would be sad and not very comforting whatsoever. On your side of the bridge-you-have-not-yet-crossed, whatever little bits of joy you can muster is from the very small soul of you, not from your enormous soul that receives unlimited joy. Settling for the small soul by hesitating to cross over, is not what you want; it's not what your heart desires, and it's not what, deep down, you know your imagined life's journey to be. Yes, you are alive. And the fact that you become so proud within your denial causes you to stay right there where you cannot move. You won't move; you just will not go forward to cross because you are afraid and unsure, like so many people around you may be. However, inside, you know you must climb that mental bridge if you truly want what's on the other side.

Draw Bridge

You can conquer and overcome any place in your mental programming by bridging the gap. Step out, with the great assurance that, at any impasse, you possess the mental equipment to ascend to a higher level of mental bridge-crossing. This idea is so explosive that no explosive can blow it up. It is invincible—ultimately impregnable—and cannot be knocked down by any person or any life circumstance. Every dream, every hope, and every bit of happiness can be yours if you follow the simple but powerful lessons of the bridge, its expansiveness, span, and reach.

You are the master builder of the mental bridge, and you can cross over in a confident way, because you know with unquestioned assurance that *you can* cross. Whatever you put great significance on will be yours: no more questioning yourself. It just cannot be otherwise and nothing in this world can stop you from obtaining it—nothing. The only thing that can stop you from crossing a bridge is you.

This ancient and truthful way has been tested by time. A bridge that stands for thousands of years is a trustworthy bridge—but only if it has been maintained, cared for, and updated.

Bridge-and-Tunnel

To acquire a self-mastery of mental bridge-crossing, it is essential to set your mindset thusly: every second, every minute, every hour, every day, every month, every year, and every decade thousands upon thousands of bridges are waiting to be crossed. To proceed along the fiery journey, every human soul, every human Fire crosses a plethora of bridges in a lifetime. Some of these bridges are small, some medium, and some are very large. But the crossings never stop, for life's terrain is one that no cartographer can map. No satellite can predict every detour, obstacle, construction site, deadlock, or traffic pattern in advance, nor can any radar bounce off the bridges that lay ahead.

Your bridge is not mine. His is not hers. Every life is designed differently, with its own journeys, and its own mental bridges to be crossed. The bridges that one person may have to cross, others may not have to. For example, you may have had a loving upbringing by parents, while another may have had none at all. The neighborhoods in which you grow up are different than someone else's; as are the people you are in contact with during your lifetime. No two people's life experiences are the same. The events of your life include some that are great and awesome, but also some that are very deep in trauma. You see, there are places in which you stand where others have not, and it's up to you to cross the bridge from where you are to where you want to go. There is no question that you are going and no question that you must cross from where you are to where you want to be.

You don't commute to work once; you commute every day. You don't cross a bridge once; you cross bridges every moment of every day. If you aren't crossing a bridge, you are stuck, treading in one place.

The secret is not locked away in a vault waiting for those select few who have a key. You have the key. Let's rephrase that: You *are* the key. What you do daily, every decision or indecision, is you crossing or uncrossing a bridge. Your daily routine can be structured in such a way as to help you break free from where you are to where you want to be, to assist you in successfully crossing over every mental bridge you encounter, in order to accomplish your Fire's purpose.

Water Under the Bridge

The daily routine—some call it the daily grind, in that you cannot ever make coffee without the grind, and you can't season a dish without first grinding the spice. Wholeness is good; but the grind of bridging makes life more whole.

Life is that simple: your daily routine delivers the potential for your joy and happiness. Pick a bridge you need to cross. Perhaps you want to graduate from college? This is a monster bridge-crossing to most everyone: not simple, alarmingly scary. It is truly not really easy. Why? Because of the understanding that you must change your daily routine to create a habit of study focus, in order to successfully complete each class. First define where you are now, mentally, then cross over that mental bridge by tweaking the matter of your daily routine. This seems so crazy to most people, but it is actually quite real: anything and everything you need is right there within your daily routine. Crossing the bridges that form in your life is just a matter of changing your daily routine to include the deeds that need to be done.

This starts when you get out of bed. The very first thing you do at the start of your day will purposefully help you accomplish the bridge-crossing. Planning a new routine for your day is paramount to creating your crossing from where you are to where you want to be.

People just hate to change their routine. Think about it: Don't you just hate adjusting to a new routine? However, recognizing this most powerful profound wisdom—that all humanity must grasp—is the single most important fact that we must believe. It will change your confidence level to such heights that you will acquire a sense of knowing and trusting, deep within yourself.

The first time they built every new bridge—think about the Brooklyn Bridge the Golden Gate Bridge, or the Chesapeake Bay Bridge over and through the water's vast expanse—it involved a change of routine. Now, crossing these bridges has become routine, the daily commute of millions. The same is true of your internal bridges. At first they are revolutionary, and then they quickly become the norm.

A great starting point is to start with something you know. Whatever challenge you choose, inject it into your daily routine every day: Do it! Let it be a part of you every day. This one thing that you do, and that you know, will bring you closer and closer to your destiny. Then, once that's part of your daily routine, pick another and then another, but do so with the understanding that this brings you closer and closer to your life's purpose. It truly is that focused, that simple, and that truthful. Every bridge-crossing begins with a step, one step forward to cross over.

Change is no different. You must step forward by changing your daily routine to include the deeds you must do, so that accomplishing these bridge-crossings becomes the habit you need to establish in order to achieve what you want. Life's everyday battles consist of what your deeds are daily. How you live each and every day—by the deeds you choose to take action on—leads right into the answers you are wanting so deeply in your life.

Rope Bridge

What is the three-ply rope that can be used to tie your life into a directional path of fulfilling your most current thoughts? The rope bridge is your habits—that's right—the habits you form that keep you stuck on one side of the bridge, or that lift you across to the other side.

A bridge is built brick by brick, cable by cable, action by action, and deed by deed. The building of the bridge is generally tedious and mundane, but the crossing of the bridge is miraculous and awe-inspiring. You have to do the former to get to the latter. It sounds obvious, only because it is. But, as we have stated, all too often the most obvious must be most stated.

A three-ply rope is so difficult to break. A rope bridge built with three-ply rope will sustain forever.

What are the three strands of your life's three-ply rope?

1) *The Blueprint:* find the map, which will guide and define and drive your purpose and inform and refine your thoughts.

2) *The System:* discover the system by which you will act and react and enact in all facets of your life.

3) *The Path*: your acts, deeds, and decisions will blaze the path of success. When you follow a higher path, you lead; when you follow a lower path, you follow. The Blueprint will teach you the higher path. The System will guide you. The Path will lead you.

With this three-ply rope, you will build an everlasting bridge and ultimately cross the great divide into your new world. For, poetically, when you cross the bridge of life, life magically becomes less cross.

~~

Drawbridge:
Draw bridges into your life, and cross them triumphantly.

CHAPTER TWELVE

Fire Light

Eyes wide open, many people are blind to what's in front of them.
Eyes closed tight, some can see for eternity.

~~

Action. Camera. Lights.

When you cannot see something, it could be for one of two reasons: one, your eyes are too weak; two, the light is too strong.

Have you ever looked into the sun? Did the sun look back? Were you blinded by the experience? Yes? Was it because your eyes were too weak or the light too strong?

Have you ever looked into a sheetrock wall? Did the sheetrock wall look back? Were you blinded by the experience? Why not?

There is a mighty difference between seeing too much and not seeing enough. The sun blinds because it is too much; sheetrock impedes your vision because it blocks. The sun overloads your sense of sight, while sheetrock underwhelms it.

Imagine that your eyes looked into the heart of the sun every moment of every day. What would you see? You would see nothing; you would be blinded by the light and would see nothing at all.

A wall of sheetrock blocks but does not blind you; a brilliant fire or a brilliant sun blinds but does not block you.

The more you see the more you are blinded. If you think you see it all, perhaps you are looking at dull surfaces. Those blessed with true vision know that what they see is only the tempered results of a fiery core. Therefore, they desire—*require*, is probably more accurate—to open their eyes, to dedicate and commit their lives to discovering the brilliance that pulses beneath the surface. True visionaries train their eyes and minds and hearts and souls to see what the fiery core looks like, to see what would otherwise blind the naked, untrained eye. Untrained, an eye is blinded by brilliance; with years of practice and diligence, an eye begins to see.

This is a monumental task, a catch-22: the fiery core is blinding—the closer you get, the less you see; if you see it, it's not the sun's core; and if you don't see it, you are blind to it. Painstaking, meticulous repetition acclimates your eyes to the intensity of the fire light.

Like the sun, more than faith is blind, faith is blinding. But without it, you cannot see.

Flash Light

A scientist first sees the surface of his or her object of study. However, the scientist wishes to see beneath the surface, to garner a glimpse of the particles blind to his naked eye. The scientist procures a microscope, and, as the name implies, scopes out the microelements of the object of study. The more micro the scientist gets, the more blinded the scientist becomes to everything else. The scientist could either step back and see the big picture, or zoom in and see specific details, but generally cannot focus on both at the same time.

The radiologist does the same with the x-ray, the programmer with a computer, and the musician with the keys or strings of an instrument. At the outset of their task, prior to delving deep, they cannot see what they want and need to see. They know it, they revel in it, and they make it their life's mission to dig in and uncover and discover the brilliant and blinding lights of life. Before they do, however, they are blind to them.

The closer you get to the sun, the less of it you can see. The closer you get to the Light, the more blinded you get. Before you begin the sedulous process of study and discovery, of acclimation and dissection, you are blind to the nuclear elements of light and life.

To understand light you must understand blindness. To understand blindness is to realize that the blind see too much, not too little. To understand blindness you must experience blindness.

Blind Test

Close your eyes. You cannot see. You cannot see these letters, nor read the words they form. But you are not blind. You can easily open your eyes and see once again.

When you close your eyes, though the darkness permeates, it engulfs more from without than from within. This is what you have always known. The words are there; not their shapes but their sounds. The words project images, never looked at but seen from within with the mind's eye. It is created, though it isn't perceived.

When your eyes are closed, every other sense is magnified. Every person, texture, and sound becomes essential to construct the universal picture.

When your eyes are closed, you see nothing but know much. From whence does your truth come? You trust in truth even though you cannot always see it. You trust that you are alive even though you cannot see life. You trust that you are breathing even though you cannot see your breath. You trust that you are, even though you cannot see that you are. You trust that there is a world around you—people, creatures, flora, fauna, minerals—even though you cannot see it and its meany details.

There is a difference between being blind and being in the dark; darkness may be abolished with light; blindness is often caused by light.

Light Reading

To take it one step further, what if your eyes were closed from the moment you were born and they did not open until this day. How would you know truth? When one is blind, how does one see truth? When one is blind, is one not blind to falsity as well?

If, from the beginning of life, one's eyes were blind to the world around, one would need to develop a deep level of trust, to trust one's other senses and trust to see through them; to trust other people and trust in their guidance and upright sight; to trust in a deeper perception and keener instinct.

A blind person's inner circle is incomparably more important than their outer circle. If, internally, the feelings and people closest are solid, the security is enchanting; if it is compromised and untrustworthy, the damage could be devastating. Inner vision, imagination, and instinct provide a certainty that manifests as personal truth. *This*, says the blind person, *is reality!*

The fact is, however, that their truth must come via base instincts, subtler senses, and people of influence. Listening, smelling, touching, feeling, emotions and intellect shape the blind person's direction and path. Without the eye and its semantic sight, everything the blind person sees, knows, feels, and holds dear is founded upon something deeper or other than molecular, biological sight.

With molecular, biological eyesight, one may compare facial and body language, one may read a person's true thoughts and feelings. Or one may be fooled by them. Memory and the spoken word, compared to seeing and observing, are less empirical for the seeing person. For the blind, they are everything, more tangible than any witnessing.

When one is blind, one reads a situation with less conflicting data: there is never a dichotomy between what you see and what you get, between what you see and what you hear, between what you see and what you believe. When one can see, one endeavors to match people's thoughts as one reads their words. The seeing person must match what a person says with a

person's body language, behaviors with words. The blind person's world is shaped not by what the blind person sees, but what the blind person knows.

Now, the ultimate question: Who is not blind from birth? Who does not have blindsides, dark corners, or unforseen consequences? Who sees all? An eye that claims to see *everything* in existence is an eye that sees *nothing* that exists.

Sure, some of us see more than others, but all of us are blind to the things beyond our eyes. Some of us are blind to physical things, some of us are blind to spiritual things, many of us are blind to the Source of all things.

Some blindness we are born with; other blindness we acquire over time. Interestingly, knowing that you are blind is the first step to seeing; remembering that you are nearsighted is the beginning to seeing far and wide; recognizing that your views are myopic allows you to begin exploring life's panorama.

Light Guide

Trust in others. More importantly, trust in yourself. Why is that you often have an easier time trusting others than you have trusting yourself? Is it because you can see others more clearly than you can see yourself? Or perhaps because you can see yourself more clearly than you can see others and are blinded by the brilliant clarity?

When you are blind you have to trust—a guide dog, a walking stick, a feeling, a friend, or a sound.

Does a person who has eyesight need to trust any less? Is there really such a thing as a seeing person? If there is, if you can see it all, why do you have to go to a computer expert to program your website? Why do you have to Google or Wikipedia a question whose answer you cannot see? Why to a mechanic to fix your car? If you can see everything, why are you blind to so many things? Why can you not see through walls, or across the globe? Why do you need a map or GPS to arrive at an unknown destination?

Why are you blind to your potential? Why are you blind to how another person feels or thinks?

Trust is essential. We are all blind. We all trust. We trust the banks— that is why they are called "trusts". We trust doctors, energy providers, the electric company, an internet provider, gasoline stations, our bosses, our employees. In life, we see very little, and we trust very much.

Light Up

Have you ever lived this way? Have you ever buried yourself in the permeating darkness? Were your eyes ever closed off to the essence? Has your perspective ever created your world, or has your world always been simply what was in front of you? Did you ever use your mind's eye, or only your eyes of flesh and blood? Have you ever created the world of your thoughts by the circumstances of events and people around you, by reading into the words and analyzing the writings, utilizing your perspective to finally arrive at a higher conclusion?

You trust that your eyes see reality, and that your ears hear what's real.

Your reality is truly developed by all you have seen and heard. How do you become absolutely sure, to be without doubt in your mind, to break free from the question realm and reach a place of knowing, that your eyes are rightly sighted, and that your ears are correctly tuned—that your understanding is correct? Are you truly seeing the real world, the absolute truth?

How do you know you are not blind? As the scientist does not know what secrets lie beneath without the microscope, how do you know what secrets lie beneath without a microscope?

As the person staring up into the sun, how do you know that you are not looking directly into the light of your life, and you are unaware—blind, blinded—because you are inundated by its sheer brilliance?

Deep down, you know that you know. The same way you know that you are alive, you know that there is more to life than what meets the naked eye; the same way you know that you breathe, you also know that there is more to life than breathing. You know what you love and what you hate; you know what is good and what is not. You know this because, in pure times, you trust in the eternal essence—the Fire—of it all.

Your Fire realizes that there are times for Prosperity, and Matter and Spirit, and Intellect, and Patterns, and Will, and Focus, and Seeding and Succeeding, and Solving and Resolving, and Heart Burn, and Bridge Building. Deep down, your Fire also knows that at a certain point, at the core, it is simply Trust.

Do you trust in your self, in your Fire? Do you trust in something beyond yourself, something cosmic, an eternal and transcendent Fire that is unseen only because it is blinding like the sun?

Like the sun, its core is unseen but its light is perceived and experienced.

You can call this trust—this faith—blind. Or you can call it blinding, awesome, and humbling. Is faith blind, or is faith blinding?

Some things are debatable, analytical, and dissectible. Other things simply are. It is your job to debate, analyze, and dissect as much of life as possible. But it is also your job to honestly accept that which transcends debate and that which cannot be dissected.

If you have to analyze and dissect the love for your parents, spouse, or children, there is something wrong. If you need a discussion to ascertain whether or not you are alive, there is something terribly wrong.

It is impossible for a human being to live in this physical sphere without ever trusting someone or something. We constantly question what is. It is natural to do so and, in fact, a good thing, a healthy thing, and a necessity. Since any relationship can devolve into a parasitic pit, full of more suspicion than suspense, we must question what is and never take anything for granted. We live in communities and peer through an eye of questioning, desperately making our reality daily.

This is a byproduct of seeing the surface and being blind to the essence. Those that are born blind to the surface do not have the luxury of distraction and know only essence. Therefore, perhaps they do not question reality as much. You see, without distortions in their way, they can see it.

Head Lights

We are all blind, literally. We are all blind even with our blessed eyesight, in that we see everything through the prism of our experiences, through our own eyes and not another's. Sure, our eyes give us another sense of perception and a tool of data collection; but just like our other tools—the mind and the heart—eyes are receptors, not processors. How we process is shaped by everything we experience. We are blind without that experience. The difference between a blind person who reads and walks, and a blind person who does neither, is the influences in his or her life. The difference between a person who uses life to create light and one who uses it to create dark, is the influences—the guide dogs, the walking sticks, the Braille—in their respective lives and what those influences teach.

Peace is born of being taught peace. Terror is born of being taught terror. Anyone that says they resort to darkness because there is no hope has been taught that you resort to darkness when there is seemingly no hope. There is also the child who resorts to light when there is seemingly no hope. When the child resorts to light, suddenly there's hope. When the child resorts to darkness, suddenly there's hopelessness.

You are blind. The question is: What type of lighthouses, light bulbs, corrective lenses, and guides do you surround yourself with, to help you process what you see?

What you learn, from your parents, teachers, friends, experiences, and environments have shaped your eyes and heart and mind to see and process the data in a certain subjective way. The flip side of how you process what you see is that this processing makes you blind to any other way of seeing or processing the raw data. I am blind to your way of thinking; you are blind to my way of seeing. Only communication—known here as Bridge Building—allows you and I to reach out and see each other's respective perspectives. Otherwise, naturally, we are blind.

Every moment of every day of every year you decide what you desire or disdain. What is passed to you allows your thoughts and intellect to choose, based on lessons from others. Your eyesight gives the choice process direction. The outcomes may be perceived in people's personalities and in their countenance. All of these created things affect you and create your own personalized, bespoke beliefs. You become a product of where you have been and what you have seen and how you have lived.

You can see only what you can see. There are billions of people on planet earth. Do you see them all? Of course not!

There are countless creatures, particles, molecules, granules, galaxies and minutia. Do you see them all? Not even close!

You are blind. At any given time, you do not see most things, but does that mean they do not exist? Of course not!

The same could be said for the parts and cells of your body. How many of your own cells, organs, sinews, ligaments, muscles, and tissues can you see? Just because you cannot see them does not mean they are not there.

What else don't you see? What else—maybe, just maybe—could be there percolating beneath the surface?

Seeing is believing? Wrong. Not seeing is believing. When you see something, you don't have to believe it. It is real (unless of course you don't trust your eyes, believing there's so much more).

How important is life—in general, and your life specifically—to you? Is life essential, non-negotiable, empirical? Is life true, absolutely true, or are you unsure? If life is true, would a false narrative ever do? Would a subjective truth ever suffice for your honest objective? Would a false object ever satisfy your truthful subject? Some may suggest that truth is not concrete, that it is relative to what you can see, or to your blindness, to your knowledge, or lack thereof. We submit that we are all blind; and that only truth is a paradigm worth looking through is one that is true for all. Not some, not many, but all.

The more you learn from others, the more ethereal material you read, the more open you are to something greater and deeper than yourself, the more you utilize *all* of your senses, in addition to the predictable ones, the more you see, the more a unifying truth begins to materialize. The less wary you are, the more aware you become: the less wary of light, the more aware of its vision

Light Bulb

You should never place a ceiling on your potential. This is cliché, but it is a

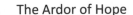
cliché that brightens and intensifies your living.

Life's ceilings could be experienced in two ways: 1) As limitations preventing you from soaring; 2) as a platform from which to suspend light bulbs.

Whether you do or do not see is less important than whether you do or do not create light. How far you see is dependent on the light bulbs at your disposal. If you surround yourself with bright people and bright ideas, you will see the world brightly and deeply. If the people and ideas in your life are dark, so will your visions and eyesight be.

The empirical world is the same world; but every single person sees and experiences that same world differently. Why? People are essentially blind, guided only by the guides and light bulbs, the sources of light— people, ideas, education, principles—in their lives. The wattage, size, and quality of the light bulbs create the differentials.

You go to a medical college to learn how to see medicine. Without the light bulb and guidelines of medical school, you are blind to medicine. You trust medical school to open the eyes of medical students, showing them what is and isn't healthy, and turn them into doctors. Many are the reasons that you trust the medical schools—reputation, results, experience, etc.—but trust you do.

Another example is sports: you know baseball is baseball because you trust to follow the rules. If a baseball league decided to change the rules—and league rules have certainly changed with the ages—then those new rule changes become the new reality. The new light bulbs and guides have been dictated.

The truth and the trust: Where do they hide, and where do they exist? Do you exist to grasp and analyze all the data, and then to make a calculation? *How can I know for certain? How can I know that this is truth; that this is not a lie?* The real world reality made from the beginning is that all eyes can see: blind or not. You want a world of no guessing; a truth to power, a truth to know, a truth to trust.

Real abundance, true peace, genuine joy—deep in your every being—that is rock solid. You can have trust that sustains your freedom, not slighted by people or persuaded otherwise by means of foolish wisdom that leads you

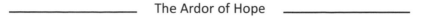

to dysfunctional dependency.

Like a light bulb: in a dark cellar it casts light; in the glaring sun it is inconsequential. How do you know whether the lights in your life are only light relative to the darkness, or are lights innately?

How to ensure that you are not blind? By being and emanating light.

Lighthouse

Light bulbs illuminate structures, buildings, and houses. Without lighting fixtures, homes remain dark . Maybe that's why they are called "fixtures": they fix the dark by casting light.

Then there is a whole other category of illumination: lighthouses, houses of light, houses whose very essence and every purpose is light. Lighthouses do not have to *be* illuminated for they *are* illumination itself.

Certain structures in your life require light bulbs to illuminate them so that their true essence may be seen. You are a Fire. You are a lighthouse. If you are blind, it is only because, like a sun, you are brilliant and blinding.

Lighthouses are created for one purpose and one purpose alone: to cast and broadcast light so as to illuminate the paths of the wayfarers, to protect the weary travelers, to guide the ships ripping through the oft-rambunctious seas of life. These lighthouses show the way with their beacons of light, warning when there is trouble afoot.

These are connected to the source of light. You are connected, and are one, with the source of light.

Light Fixture

At all times, there is something you cannot see, guiding and lighting you with righteousness. It pursues you, hounds you, like life itself. And yet, although the abstract power pulls and pushes you and is as real as reality itself, you are unsure of its definition and dimension. You cannot touch it; mostly you fight it. But you know it is there: an unseen power of truth. It moves and shakes you to negate the bad and seek the good. Every person recognizes this unseen power. It resonates. It permeates. It inculcates.

If you look at yourself honestly, you know when you are illuminating and illuminated, and when you are blocked in and blacked out.

Fooling yourself is a whole other type of blindness, not caused by blinding light but by closing your eyes. And a blindness caused by closed windows can easily be remedied by simply opening them up again.

Blindside

Wherever there is light, there is also shadow. Without light there is no shadow. When you cook, there is waste; when you plant flowers, weeds sprout up. Dark shadows are a byproduct of light.

They create a dark side, a blind side. Whenever there is light in you, there is also a shadow that claims the light to be false.

There is truth, real honest truth in it and it is before you, inside you, and guides you to do good always. But why? Where does it come from? Why does it hunt you down and pester you to acknowledge it? With strong light comes strong shadows, powerful opposition to the light. With a healthy illuminated mind comes a healthy ego, one that tries to rationalize everything and put you at the center, even at the expense of the light source.

The light shines brilliantly, so blindingly that you are empowered to walk into its warm embrace and do light, do good, and do right. Then the other voice—the self-centered, egotistical voice—scratches in a gravely rasp: *Stay in the shadows. Stay away from the light. It will blind you.*

The stronger the light, the stronger the shadowy presence, the stronger the raspy voice.

The shadow blindsides you, not with light but with a blindfold. Light is blinding; but the shadow is blindsiding. The difference is: one blindness is caused by too much light, while the other blindness is caused by too little light.

The shadow is not someone outside of yourself. It is your ego, your self-centeredness, your subjectivity, and your biology raging against your transcendence. In and of itself, the shadow isn't bad; it has its place. It is only negative if it tries to keep you from the light instead of accentuating it. The shadow has one job: to magnify, accentuate, define, stress, and emphasize the light. As makeup eye shadow emphasizes one's eyes, light shadow should emphasize one's light.

Do not ignore the shadows; use them. Do not ignore your selfishness, your self-centeredness; use it to accent your power and accentuate your shine, to magnify your sun and spread your rays, to highlight your ability and cast its brilliant rays.

Light Source

What is the source of Light? What is its name? Does it even have a name? If yes, who named it? If not, what should we call it?

Initially, Light would seem like an appropriate and natural name. The problem with this, however, is that the existence of Light assumes and presumes a source that creates and casts the Light. Maybe we should call it Light Source.

Or simply: Source. Light Source. Fire Source. Intellect Source. Bridge Source. Matter and Spirit Source. Focus Source. Heart Source. Patterns Source. Seed and Harvest Source. Light Source. Prosperity Source. Will Source. Bridge Source.

Find the voice written in this finite world by the infinite. Look for the Source and you find everything; look for everything and you may not find the Source. Unveil the brilliance within the face of existence. Truth and light does not exist to please humanity, but humanity lives to share truth and cast light.

Search for and discover the one thing that finds the commonality in all things, not the many things that find the differences in one thing. We can all live at a level that demands a truth deeper than a surface, a truth rooted in the Source. Aspire to the one thing you can trust, and that can help you decide on anything. Desire and demand to see, to hear, to read the scroll of

The Garden

Bulbs—light bulbs and flower bulbs.

This garden you are preparing is so rich with foliage that you must dig richly into the earth and plant, prune, and harvest it. And when you do, its inner potential begins to bloom, and you along with it.

Yet, even as you seek the creation, the creation seeks to hide from its Creator. Hide and seek: even as you seek it hides; even as you open your eyes, it blinds—even as you seek to see, it seems to cease.

Fierce is the pull; magnetism is too weak a description for a force so powerful. Ironically, the more you look for something the less of it you see. Then, suddenly, when you close your eyes and are about to nod off, exhausted from your exhaustive search, you suddenly see it.

Hiding is a good thing. Energy revealed is energy that is weak.

This supreme power exists in such a mighty way it overwhelms you to surrender into being congruently aligned in right order to this light that illuminates you all to allow your divine soul to catch fire and burn with love towards this source.

With eyes closed to reality, you see dirt brown earth; with eyes open, you envision a flourishing garden.

In the dark places, the shadowy darkness, the light begins to seep through. Through the cracks in the hard shell, glimmers of hope crawl through like newborn children with gleeful expressions.

The light shines beneath the soil, the soiled earth, as it does in the blooming flowers.

Suddenly you are Blinded By The Light — and, as you look back retrospectively, from destination back to point of departure, you can finally see the journey in its entirety: Fire Light to Bridge Building, Heart Burn to Solving and Resolving, Seed and Succeed to Focus, Will to Patterns, Intellect to Matter and Spirit, Prosperity to Fire.

The tillers of the garden, those who plant through blood, sweat, and tears, cultivate a home, a dwelling where the Fire, unleashed, can reside. When you learn to open your eyes, even the most brilliant Light will not blind you.

The Fire within you is the Fire within all. The Fire within all is the Fire of the world.

You see, when you learn to become brilliant, the brilliance doesn't blind; it illuminates. When you remember that you are Fire, you don't get burned. When you burn, you sing, without ever singeing.

When different flames are placed together they reveal themselves as one greater fire. Oneness and unity is the ultimate test if what you see is dark coal or bright light.

Your free will gives you the greatest power here and now, created for you by that which could never be described by the mere words of human deficiency. We all—humans imbued with Fire and created in Its fiery image— we all have a spark of the Fire burning bright and eternally. And we can all ask the questions that will ultimately answer our future here and now, but indefinitely for our souls.

What is truth? What do I see? Whom do I trust?

Does such a reality exist?

It does.

It is what you see when you open your eyes.

It is called: *The Ardor of Hope.*

~~

Closing your eyes to darkness allows you to open them to light.

reality, a manifesto that pierces deep and pieces together the innermost being of yourself, so that you may ultimately read the world and, more to the point, your own fiery self.

Open your eyes not to a reality based on all other human-guided cues that try to persuade you in this world according to their Ego-based "truth" of what is right. What they might covet is the wrong advice for you. You need a written word to trust and love, that you live continuously. Time-tested and true, give us not the young wine of coarse vines, but the aged vintage of thousands of years in the making: mature yet cutting-edge, timeless yet timely, dizzyingly potent yet lucidly clearheaded, originating from the unseen-yet-all-seeing, blinding-yet-neve-blind power that controls and ignites all the known and unknown universes.

Where does it exist, and how certain is it? Can this prove truth into existence, or existence into truth?

The Firelight

Does a fire get burned? If you are light you cannot be blind.

It is so important to know that this unseen entity lets the universe live. The Source continually creates the cosmos—continually continually continually continually, sourcing and resourcing.

The prime mover of this world—the Cosmic Fire, the Source—burns in this world precisely because it is the desired hearth of the Cosmic Fire. The Fire gives of Itself, perpetually, and pursues every living soul constantly, never ceasing, only magnifying and increasing. That is what Fire does. The unseen power humbly and persistently draws us in—patiently, kindly, and lovingly following our errant moves of our own personal free wills, to bring us closer and closer, but without ever getting burned.
If you know where to look, you can see the Fire, the light and its Source, the Truth. But, like the core of the sun, the Source of existence—the Source of the light—remains hidden behind the veil of all creation. The Fire seeps out but does not unleash lest it devour, blind, and conflagrate. Its power is solidified by its concealment: things revealed are things superficial; things seen are things external. As one cannot see a soul, one cannot see the Fire. If one can, it is not Fire.